How to Survive the Death of an Adult Child

A Guide to Coping with Profound Sorrow,
Navigate the Journey of Grief and Healing,
Embrace Life After Unimaginable Loss

By G.M. Grace

Contents

Dedication

To my beloved Aaron and Bobby, whose lives were cut short but whose spirits remain with us always. Your memories are cherished deeply, and your presence is forever missed.

To my sister, Shelly, whose incredible strength and resilience have inspired me in the face of unimaginable loss. I began writing this book when we lost Aaron, but the overwhelming grief forced me to put it away. Years later, when Bobby passed, I knew I had to finish it for you. This book is dedicated to you, Shelly, in the hope that it offers some solace and guidance as you navigate the profound sorrow of losing your two adult children.

Your courage and unwavering love for Aaron and Bobby have been a testament to the power of a mother's heart. This book is written with all my love and in honor of your enduring spirit. May it help you find a way to embrace life and heal, even as you carry the weight of their absence.

Introduction

In the early morning hours of a chilly October day, I received a phone call that would change our lives forever. The voice on the other end was trembling, delivering the heartbreaking news that my nephew Aaron had passed away. The world seemed to stand still as the weight of this loss settled into my heart. Aaron was more than just a nephew; he was a vibrant soul who filled our lives with joy, laughter, and boundless energy. His absence left a void that felt insurmountable.

In the days and weeks that followed, I watched my sister Shelly navigate the unimaginable grief of losing her child. Her strength and resilience in the face of such profound sorrow were nothing short of extraordinary. She became a pillar for our family, even as she carried the heaviest burden of all. During this time, I began to write, hoping to capture the raw emotions and experiences that we were all grappling with. Writing became a way to process the pain, and I started to craft a guide for others who might face the same devastating loss.

But as the months turned into years, the manuscript remained unfinished. The grief was too overwhelming, and life had a way of moving forward, even when it felt like time should stand still. The manuscript was tucked away, gathering dust, a painful reminder of a chapter in our lives that we were still struggling to understand.

Then, a few years later, another call came, bringing with it a new wave of sorrow. My nephew Bobby, Aaron's younger brother, had also passed away. The shock and grief that followed were even more profound, as if the wounds from Aaron's loss had been ripped open anew.

Watching my sister endure the loss of her second child was heart-wrenching. Shelly's strength was tested in ways that no one should ever have to experience.

It was during this time that I knew I had to return to the manuscript. The story wasn't just about coping with grief; it was about survival, resilience, and the enduring strength of a mother's love. I wrote with renewed purpose, hoping to offer some measure of comfort and guidance to Shelly and to anyone else who might be navigating the same treacherous path.

This book is a testament to the love and memory of Aaron and Bobby. It is also a tribute to Shelly's incredible strength and her unwavering determination to keep moving forward, even when the pain seemed too much to bear. Through this book, I hope to provide solace and support to other parents who have faced the unthinkable, and to remind them that they are not alone.

As you read these pages, know that every word is written with love, empathy, and a deep understanding of the journey through grief. My hope is that this book will help you find a way to navigate your sorrow, embrace the memories of your loved ones, and discover a path to healing and renewal.

Chapter 1: Understanding the Waves of Grief

A Story of Immediate Loss

It was a cold, grey morning when Susan's phone rang. The shrill sound shattered the early morning silence, jolting her from her sleep. Groggily, she answered, only to be met with the trembling voice of her daughter-in-law. The words were muffled, choked by sobs, but the message was clear: her son, Michael, had passed away in a tragic accident.

For a moment, Susan couldn't process what she was hearing. It felt surreal, like a scene from a nightmare she desperately wanted to wake up from. Michael, her vibrant, loving son, was gone. The shock was a tidal wave, sweeping away her breath and leaving her numb.

Susan sat on the edge of her bed, the phone still in her hand, unable to move. Her husband, Jack, stirred beside her, sensing something was wrong. When she finally found the words to tell him, his look of horror and disbelief mirrored her own.

Susan felt like she was moving through a fog in the following hours. She made the necessary phone calls to family members and close friends, each conversation feeling like a dagger to her heart. Every word she spoke seemed to make the loss more real, more permanent.

The house began to fill with people offering condolences, their voices a distant hum in the background of her shattered reality.

Her emotions were a storm, raging and unpredictable. One moment, she was angry and furious at the universe for taking Michael away. The next, she was consumed by a crushing sadness, the weight of her grief making it hard to breathe. There were moments of denial, where she almost believed he would walk through the door, his familiar smile lighting up the room.

Through it all, Susan tried to focus on the practical tasks. She knew she had to make arrangements for Michael's funeral, a task that seemed insurmountable in her state of grief. Her friends and family were a lifeline, stepping in to help with the details and providing a shoulder to cry on. Their support was a small comfort in the midst of the overwhelming pain.

Despite the chaos, Susan knew she needed to take care of herself. She forced herself to eat, drink water, and rest, even though it felt like the hardest thing in the world. Her body was exhausted, but sleep was elusive. Her mind raced with memories of Michael and the unbearable reality of his absence.

In those first 24 hours, Susan allowed herself to feel everything. She cried until she had no tears left, screamed into the void, and sat silently, lost in her thoughts. She knew that this was just the beginning of a long, painful journey through grief, but she also knew that she had to face it head-on.

The news that your adult child has passed away strikes with the force of a tsunami, leaving behind a landscape of grief that seems impossible. This chapter invites you to understand and navigate the initial tumultuous hours and days following such devastating news. Grief may feel like an uncharted ocean, but recognizing and understanding your emotions and reactions can serve as a compass, helping you steer through the darkest waters toward a place of gradual healing.

1.1 When the Unthinkable Happens: The First 24 Hours

Emotional Whirlwind

The first moments after receiving the heartbreaking news are often marked by an intense emotional whirlwind. You might find yourself in a state of shock, disbelief, or numbness, unable to grasp the reality of what has occurred. This numbness, often the mind's temporary shield against intense pain, can be confusing and disorienting. It's important to understand that these reactions are natural protective responses of the human psyche trying to cope with acute emotional distress. They do not signify a lack of feeling but rather an overwhelming influx of emotion that your mind is trying to process. During these initial hours, giving yourself permitting discussing your feelings, reminiscing about your child, or simply sitting together in silence, the presence of someone who cares can help mitigate the experience of these feelings without judgment, which is crucial to your emotional well-being.

Immediate Responses

In the wake of such news, reaching out to a close friend or family member can provide an essential anchor. Human connection during a profound loss can be powerful, offering emotional support and helping you navigate the practical aspects that follow a sudden loss—emotional support and help you. Choosing someone who will listen without urging you to move past your grief before you are ready is a necessary essential isolation that often accompanies grief.

Practical Considerations

The reality of losing an adult child brings with it a cascade of immediate decisions that need to be made, from informing other family members to handling your child's affairs. This can seem daunting when you are already grappling with emotional turmoil. It is here that the value of asking for help becomes evident. Delegate tasks where possible, and don't hesitate to lean on relatives, friends, or professionals for support with arrangements. Remember, asking for help is not a sign of weakness but a necessary step in managing the practical realities during this time, allowing you to focus on your emotional response and begin grieving.

Self-Compassion

One of the most crucial aspects during the first 24 hours is practicing self-compassion. Grieving is as individual as it is universal. There is no "right way" to experience loss, and there is no standard timeline for grief. Allow yourself to feel whatever you are feeling without self-criticism. Some may find themselves crying uncontrollably, while others might not cry at all. Each response is valid. Grant yourself the kindness and patience you would offer a friend. It's okay to be not okay during this profoundly difficult time.

Reflection Section

To aid in your journey of grief, consider taking a moment to reflect on and write down what you are feeling and experiencing. This can be a way to begin processing the emotions that might seem overwhelming right now. Write about your immediate thoughts, fears, and the support you wish to have in the coming days. This journaling can be a small, therapeutic step in acknowledging and facing your grief.

1.2 Recognizing Grief's Physical Toll and Self-Care Necessities

Grief, while profoundly emotional, also manifests physically in ways that can be both surprising and debilitating. It is not uncommon to experience a range of physical symptoms that include exhaustion, changes in appetite, sleep disturbances, and a host of other bodily reactions. These symptoms are not merely discomfort; they are the physical expressions of your psychological pain and must be addressed with equal seriousness. Exhaustion can be all-encompassing, making even the simplest tasks feel insurmountable. This isn't just tiredness—it's a deep, bone-weary drain that depletes your energy at every level. Changes in appetite can also occur; some might find themselves unable to eat, while others might turn to food for comfort, neither of which is beneficial in the long term. Sleep, too, can become elusive or too abundant, disrupting natural rhythms and leading to a cycle of fatigue that hinders the healing process.

Self-care during this time is not just beneficial; it is necessary for your well-being. It's crucial to prioritize practices supporting your physical health, such as staying hydrated, eating nutritious foods, and maintaining a regular sleep schedule. Hydration helps manage fatigue and keeps your body functioning correctly despite your reduced appetite or increased stress levels. Nutrition plays a critical role, too; opting for balanced meals can help stabilize your mood and energy levels. While cooking may seem like a daunting task, simple meals that require minimal preparation or the support of family members or friends to prepare food can ensure you are nourished. Regarding rest, while sleep may not come quickly, creating a calming bedtime routine can help. This might include reading, listening to soothing music, or practicing gentle yoga or meditation to encourage your body to relax and invite sleep.

At times, the physical symptoms of grief can be intense enough to mimic or trigger medical conditions, making it difficult to know when to seek professional health advice. It is essential to consult a healthcare provider if you experience persistent physical symptoms that do not improve with basic self-care measures or if you have pre-existing conditions that cause the stress of grief to worsen. Symptoms such as prolonged insomnia, significant weight loss or gain, or severe energy depletion are signals that professional medical advice is needed. A healthcare provider can offer treatment and guidance on managing these symptoms effectively.

Crafting a personal self-care plan is a proactive step toward managing the physical aspects of grief. This plan should include daily goals for hydration, nutrition, and sleep, as well as regular check-ins with yourself to assess what is working and what isn't. Additionally, gentle physical activity, like walks or light stretching, can improve your physical well-being and provide a mental break from your grief. It's also helpful to set reminders for these activities, as grief can make it easy to forget your care needs. Remember, the goal of this plan is not to add pressure but to create a structure that supports your health during a tumultuous time. This plan can also evolve as you move through different stages of grief, adapting to your changing needs and circumstances.

By acknowledging and attending to the physical manifestations of your grief, you are taking essential steps towards healing—not just in the mind but also in the body.

1.3 The Rollercoaster of Emotions: What's Normal?

When grappling with the loss of an adult child, you embark on an emotional odyssey that can feel as if you're perpetually riding a rollercoaster, one moment up in the realms of poignant memories, the next plummeting into the depths of despair. This spectrum of emotions— from anger, guilt, and disbelief to moments of relief or fleeting peace—

is entirely normal. Understanding and accepting the breadth and variability of these emotions are vital in your healing process. It's natural to feel anger, perhaps towards circumstances surrounding your child's passing, or frustration at the world for continuing as though nothing has changed. Guilt may weave through your thoughts as you ponder the 'what ifs' and the 'if onlys'. You are acknowledging these feelings and understanding that they are common reactions, not indictments of your character or a reflection of your love is crucial.

The intensity with which you experience these emotions can vary daily, but from moment to moment. It's akin to weathering a storm: one minute, the sea is calm, and the next, you're battling gale-force winds. Managing these intense emotions requires a toolkit of adaptable strategies when you feel overwhelmed. Breathwork, for instance, can serve as an anchor, helping to ground your emotions. When a wave of grief hits hard, taking a moment to focus on deep, steady breaths can help manage the immediacy of the pain. Additionally, setting aside specific times during the day to reflect on your feelings can provide a structured way to process emotions without letting them dominate your entire day. This could be a mourning journal session where you externalize your thoughts and fears or an evening walk where you reflect on the day and the feelings it stirred.

Finding healthy ways to express these emotions is crucial in navigating them. Journaling offers a private, unfiltered medium to converse with your feelings and argue with or plead with them without fear of judgment. For some, physical expression—such as running, yoga, or other forms of exercise—releases pent-up emotions, channeling them into physical activity that exhausts the body but calms the mind. Art, too, allows for a transformative expression of grief, turning pain into purpose through creation, whether it be painting, music, writing, or any form of creative art that resonates with you. These activities help in expressing emotions and understanding them, giving them form and dimension that can be seen, felt, or heard, making them easier to confront and manage.

Equally important is emotional support from friends, family, or counselors. Connecting with others who acknowledge your pain and allow you to express your emotions without fear of judgment builds a supportive network around you. Sometimes, sharing your feelings with another person can help lighten the emotional load, making it more bearable. It also opens up avenues for receiving compassion and empathy, which can be incredibly soothing during intense grief. If the emotions become too overwhelming, turning to professional counselors or therapists who specialize in grief can provide the guided support needed to navigate through them. These professionals can offer strategies tailored to your needs, helping you understand and manage your emotions in a safe, supportive environment.

In this tumultuous phase, remember that every emotion you experience is valid, and each has its place in the tapestry of your grief. There is no right or wrong way to feel, and there is certainly no timetable for when certain emotions should or should not appear. The process is deeply personal, and allowing yourself to feel these emotions entirely is a step toward healing, not away from it.

1.4 Immediate Coping Strategies: From Breathing to Support Networks

In the storm of emotions that follows the loss of an adult child, finding immediate, practical strategies to manage the overwhelming moments becomes crucial. These strategies are not about moving on from your grief but finding ways to navigate it with grace and resilience. Breathing techniques are among the most straightforward yet powerful tools at your disposal. These can serve as quick anchors, pulling you back from the precipice of overwhelming sadness or panic. A primary but effective method is the deep breathing technique, often called diaphragmatic breathing. Here, you focus on slowly inhaling through your nose, allowing your lungs to fill, and then exhaling equally through slightly pursed lips. This type of breathing helps reduce the 'fight or flight' response, calming your nervous system and bringing your focus back to the present moment. It's beneficial in acute stress, providing a quick way to regain control over your emotions, making it a valuable tool in your immediate coping arsenal.

Building a support network is another cornerstone of navigating your grief. The people within this network can offer emotional buffering, practical help, and the simple yet profound gift of presence. When assembling your support network, consider including individuals with various strengths and perspectives. This might include close family members who share your loss, friends who offer emotional understanding, and professionals like counselors or spiritual advisors who can provide expert guidance. It's essential to communicate your needs clearly with your support network—let them know what type of support you find helpful, whether it's having someone to talk to when you're feeling low, help with everyday tasks, or space when you need solitude. Remember, the people in your life may want to help but might not know how or what you would find most beneficial unless you tell them. Communication here is critical—not just for expressing your needs but also for setting expectations on how often and in what ways you feel comfortable receiving support.

Amidst the chaos that grief can bring to your daily life, maintaining some semblance of routine can provide a crucial sense of normalcy. A routine doesn't mean a rigid schedule that stresses you out but rather a gentle structure to your day that helps you anchor yourself. This might include setting regular mealtimes, incorporating a short walk in the morning or evening, or setting aside time for activities you find soothing, such as reading or gardening. These activities aren't meant to distract you from your grief but to give you a framework within which you can function, which is especially helpful on days when grief feels all-consuming. The predictability of a routine can help to mitigate the feeling of groundlessness that often accompanies the early stages of grieving.

Finally, setting boundaries is essential to managing how you navigate spaces and relationships during your grieving process. It's healthy and necessary to set limits on how much you engage with others, how you participate in social or work activities, and what kind of conversations you are ready to have about your loss. You might find that specific social settings or well-meaning but intrusive questions can trigger profound sadness or distress; it's okay to express to others that you are not ready to discuss specific topics or to attend certain events. It's also okay to ask for privacy when you need it or to choose not to engage in discussions about your grief until you feel more capable of handling it. Setting these boundaries can help protect your emotional space, giving you the room to breathe and move through your grief at your own pace.

You can create a framework that supports your day-to-day journey through grief through these strategies—breathing techniques to manage acute moments of distress, building a supportive network, maintaining a comforting routine, and setting necessary boundaries. Each of these strategies empowers you to face the complexities of loss with a sense of preparedness and agency. Remember, while the path of grief is profoundly personal, you need not walk it alone.

Chapter 2: Rituals of Remembrance and Goodbye

A Story of Rituals of Remembrance

When Emily received the devastating news that her daughter, Sarah, had passed away unexpectedly, she felt as if her world had come to a standstill. Sarah, with her infectious laughter and boundless energy, had been the light of Emily's life. The thought of a world without her seemed unbearable.

In the initial days of shock and grief, Emily struggled to find a way to honor Sarah's memory. The idea of planning a memorial felt both overwhelming and necessary. She wanted to create a tribute that truly reflected the essence of who Sarah was—a vibrant, compassionate, and spirited young woman.

Emily began by reflecting on what made Sarah unique. She remembered her daughter's love for music, particularly how she would play her guitar and sing her heart out. Music had always been a central part of Sarah's life, bringing joy to everyone

*around her. Emily decided incorporating music into
the memorial would be a fitting way to honor her
daughter's passion.*

*She reached out to Sarah's friends, who were
musicians, and asked if they would perform at the
memorial service. They gladly agreed, each eager to
contribute a piece that had special meaning. Emily
also curated a playlist of Sarah's favorite songs
throughout the service, ensuring her presence would
be felt through the music she loved.*

*As she continued to plan, Emily thought about
Sarah's love for nature. Sarah had always felt a deep
connection to the outdoors, often spending her
weekends hiking and exploring local parks. Emily
decided to hold the memorial service in Sarah's
favorite park, under a large oak tree, where they had
shared many picnics and long conversations.*

*To personalize the memorial further, Emily
invited friends and family to share their memories of
Sarah. She set up a memory board where guests could
pin photos, notes, and small mementos that reminded
them of her. During the service, several of Sarah's
closest friends and family members stood up to share*

stories and anecdotes, painting a vivid picture of her life and the impact she had on those around her.

Emily also wanted to create a lasting tribute to Sarah's memory. She planted a tree in the park where the memorial was held, a living reminder of her daughter's spirit and love for nature. She chose a cherry blossom tree, knowing that its beautiful blooms would symbolize hope and renewal each spring.

Involving others in planning helped Emily feel supported and less alone in her grief. It also allowed those who loved Sarah to contribute meaningfully, creating a collective space for mourning and remembrance. The memorial became a community effort, a testament to the many lives Sarah had touched.

Emily found comfort in these acts of remembrance. They turned her grief into a creative, cathartic expression of love, allowing her to honor Sarah in a way that felt deeply personal and true to her spirit. The memorial was not just a goodbye; it was a celebration of Sarah's life, filled with laughter, music, and the beauty of nature—everything she had cherished.

In the quiet moments when the world seems to pause in respect for your grief, you might find yourself pondering how best to honor the vibrant life your child lived. A memorial serves not only as a farewell but as a profound expression of love, capturing the essence of a life that continues to echo in the hearts of those it touched. Planning a memorial can be a profoundly personal, therapeutic process, helping you and your loved ones articulate and celebrate your child's unique legacy. It's a journey through memory, a crafted homage that says, "Here lived a wonderful soul who will always be remembered."

Planning a Memorial That Honors Your Child's Legacy

2.1 Personalizing the Memorial

Creating a memorial that truly reflects your child's personality and interests can be a comforting act, turning grief into a creative, cathartic expression of love. Start by considering what made your child unique—perhaps their passion for music, love for the outdoors, or unrelenting sense of humor. Think about incorporating these elements into the memorial. For a music lover, you might organize a playlist of their favorite songs during the service or have musicians perform live. If they were an avid reader, consider readings from their favorite books or poems that resonate with their life story. For someone who loves nature, hosting the memorial in a beloved park or garden, perhaps during their favorite time of year, can add a deeply personal touch. The key is to weave their essence into every detail, making the memorial reflect their life and what they cherished.

Involving Others

Remember, memorials are also for the living—a chance for friends and family to gather, offer support, and share memories. Involving others in the planning and execution can be a way to collectively process the loss and celebrate the life of your child. Encourage friends and family to contribute their ideas or share special memories during the service. This could be through speeches, storytelling sessions, or a memory board where attendees can pin photos, notes, or tokens that remind them of their child. Such contributions enrich the memorial and help build a support network, reinforcing the notion that you are not alone in your grief.

Alternative Memorial Ideas

Traditional memorials are not the only way to honor a loved one. Alternative memorials can be equally poignant and perhaps even more reflective of your child's impact and personality. Consider a memorial such as planting a tree or a garden in their memory—an enduring, living tribute that grows and changes with the seasons. Alternatively, organizing a charity fundraiser or a volunteer day in their name can be a powerful way to extend their legacy of kindness and compassion. Such events memorialize your child and create a positive impact in the world, a beautiful testament to their life.

Memorializing Digital Presence

In today's digital age, many people live vibrant online lives, and your child may have been one of them. Managing their digital legacy is an essential aspect of modern memorials. This might involve maintaining their social media pages as a place for friends and family to gather and share memories. Some platforms offer options to memorialize accounts, which keeps the profile visible while preventing anyone from logging into the account. Creating an online memorial website or a digital guestbook can also provide a space for expressions of condolence and remembrance from those who might not be able to attend a physical memorial service. These digital spaces offer a unique way to compile stories, photos, and videos celebrating your child's life. They provide a lasting virtual space where their memory can continue to touch lives.

Interactive Element: Reflection Section

Consider writing a brief passage about what your child loved most or a favorite memory you shared. Reflect on how this could be incorporated into a memorial or how you might use this memory to help others remember your child. This personal reflection can serve as a grounding activity, helping you connect with the joyous moments you spent together and may inspire ideas for personalizing their memorial.

As you plan a memorial, whether it be traditional or unique, remember that this ritual is as much for you as it is for those who share your loss. It's a step toward healing, a way to externalize your grief and affection, and a celebration of a life that, though no longer present in your body, continues to inspire and influence the world in profound ways. Through these acts of remembrance and goodbye, you not only honor your child's legacy but also carve a path toward your healing, surrounded by the love and memories that bind you to the child you cherished.

2.2 Private Rituals of Remembrance for the Family

Creating intimate spaces and practices within the comfort of your home offers a tender way to remember and celebrate your child's life in your daily environment. These personal rituals and spaces constantly remind you of their presence in your life and provide a sanctuary where emotions can be freely expressed and cherished memories preserved.

Creating a Memory Space

Designating a specific area in your home to honor your child can transform a part of your living space into a sacred corner that holds their essence. This doesn't need to be elaborate; it can be as simple as dedicating a shelf or a small table where you display photos of your child, their favorite books, perhaps a few cherished possessions that were dear to them, or even their artworks or hand-written notes. You might add items that evoke personal memories, such as souvenirs from places you visited together or gifts they gave you. This space can be a focal point for your remembrance, where you can feel close to them, speak with them, or reflect in silence. Enhancing this space with comforting elements such as candles or a small lamp can create a warm, inviting atmosphere that beckons you to linger, remember, and connect with the love you shared.

Rituals in Daily Life

Integrating small yet meaningful rituals into your daily life can help maintain a sense of connection with your child. Start a tradition of starting your day by saying good morning to them at their memory space or end your day with a goodnight wish. You might play their favorite song each morning or prepare their favorite weekend dish. On more challenging days, when their absence feels too heavy, these rituals can bring significant comfort and a feeling of ongoing connection. These acts don't need to be grand; their power lies in their significance – in how they echo the love and the bond you shared. Over time, these rituals can evolve or change as you find new ways to embody and remember the relationship in your daily life.

2.3 Writing a Remembrance

Writing letters to your child can be a powerful, personal practice to articulate feelings that are hard to express otherwise. It's a way to continue the conversation with them, to share your daily joys and sorrows, or to update them on family news just as you might have done before. These letters can be kept in a journal, added to the memory space, or even read aloud. Writing can bridge the gap between past and present, keeping your child's memory vibrant and integral to your life. It also serves as a valuable outlet for your grief, allowing you to pour your heart on paper, which can be incredibly therapeutic.

Family Remembrance Activities

Engaging in activities as a family can be a comforting way to remember and honor your loved one collectively. Consider establishing a routine, perhaps a monthly family dinner, where each member shares a story or a memory of your child. You could also work together on a project your child would have loved, like crafting a family scrapbook of favorite memories or working on a charity project in their honor. During holidays or special occasions, involve your child's memory by creating a new tradition that includes their memory, such as lighting a unique candle or displaying a photo in a prominent place during family gatherings. These activities help keep your child's memory alive and strengthen family bonds, providing shared space for grief and remembrance.

These private rituals and spaces create a framework for your grief, allowing you to express it in ways that feel right to you, at your own pace, and in your own space. They serve as gentle reminders of your child's life and legacy, woven into the fabric of your everyday existence, ensuring that their memory continues to live on in the most personal and profound ways.

The Importance of Memorial Objects and Spaces

Memorial objects and spaces connect to the memories and legacy of a child who has passed. These items and places can become sacred touchpoints, offering comfort and a physical way to honor and remember a deeply cherished life. Keepsakes, whether they are items your child owned, gifts they gave, or new items chosen to symbolize their life, carry profound emotional weight. Selecting or creating these keepsakes can be a deeply personal process that involves sifting through memories and selecting the physical items that resonate most strongly with the love and experiences shared.

Keepsakes and mementos are more than just objects; they are vessels of memories, each holding a story, a moment, or a feeling. As you choose keepsakes, think about those items that bring a vivid memory to life—the watch they wore daily, a favorite book, or even a simple collection of photographs. You might also consider creating new keepsakes, such as a quilt made from their clothes, a piece of jewelry that incorporates their birthstone, or even a custom piece of art that depicts a significant aspect of their life. Each of these items carries a piece of your child's story, serving as a physical manifestation of your memories that you can see, touch, and hold close when words are too hard to find.

Creating a memorial garden is another beautiful way to honor your child in a living, thriving space that can provide solace and reflection. Choose a quiet spot in your garden or find a community garden where you can dedicate a space. Plant flowers, shrubs, or trees that are meaningful to your child or that bloom in their favorite colors. Incorporate elements that speak to their nature—perhaps stones or a water feature for someone who loved the outdoors or sculptural elements that reflect their interests or passions. As the garden grows and changes with the seasons, it offers a living tribute that memorializes their life and symbolizes the ongoing nature of love beyond physical presence.

The concept of a memory box can also be a comforting way to collect and preserve smaller keepsakes and mementos. This box can be filled with items like ticket stubs from concerts you attended together, letters or cards they wrote, small gifts they gave you, or even random trinkets that remind you of shared moments or jokes. Decorating the box itself can be a part of the healing process—perhaps painting it, lining it with fabric from their clothing, or adorning it with photos. Choosing what goes into the box and arranging these items can be a therapeutic way to engage with your memories, providing a private, personal space that holds the essence of your child's spirit.

Exploring the idea of tattoos or custom art offers a more permanent form of remembrance. A tattoo is a deeply personal choice that can serve as a daily reminder of the bond you shared. It might be their favorite quote, a symbol that represents something they loved, or even a simple, meaningful design that reminds you of them. For those who prefer a less permanent option, commissioning a piece of art can be equally meaningful. This might be a portrait, an abstract piece that captures their essence, or a custom sculpture. Like tattoos, these art pieces create a lasting legacy that can be seen daily, reminding you of the love and connection that endures.

Each memorial object and space offers a unique way to remember and honor your child. Whether through small, handheld souvenirs that you can carry with you, a garden where you can sit and reflect, a memory box filled with tangible pieces of their life, or a piece of art that captures their spirit, these memorials serve as profound expressions of love. They stand as testaments to a life that, though no longer present in the physical realm, continues to inspire, influence, and resonate in the physical spaces and objects we hold dear. Through these acts of remembrance, we find a way to keep our connection to our child alive and a path to healing that honors their memory in tangible, meaningful ways.

2.4 Navigating Anniversaries and Birthdays Early On

Anniversaries, birthdays, and significant dates that resonate with memories of your child can often feel like emotional landmarks, each carrying its unique set of challenges and emotions. Preparing for these days can help manage the emotional turbulence they often bring. One effective strategy is to acknowledge ahead of time that these days will be difficult and to plan accordingly. This might mean taking the day off work, ensuring you don't have an overly busy schedule, or even planning a quiet day for reflection. It's also helpful to think about how you want to spend these days. Some find comfort in solitude, while others may prefer the company of close friends or family who understand their loss.

Creating new traditions on these significant dates can serve as a powerful means of honoring your child's memory while acknowledging their absence's ongoing impact. The idea is to find a balance that respects the gravity of the day but also allows space for remembrance and joy. For example, if your child has a favorite place, such as a park or a cafe, visiting this place on their birthday or the anniversary of their passing can become a cherished new tradition. Alternatively, you might start a ritual of releasing biodegradable lanterns or planting flowers each year on these dates. These acts can create a sense of continuity and connection, providing a structured opportunity to celebrate your child's life and spirit meaningfully and personally.

During these times, the support of friends, family, or a community who understands your loss is invaluable. Please tell your support network how you feel as these significant dates approach and let them know how they can best support you. This might involve them being physically present, helping organize a remembrance activity, or simply giving you space if needed. Remember, it's okay to express what you need—those who care for you will want to support you in the best way they can. It's also beneficial to connect with support groups, either in person or online, where you can share your feelings and experiences with others navigating similar grief paths. These connections can provide comfort and reassurance that you are not alone in your sorrow and remembrance.

Balancing grief with the celebration of your child's life on these significant dates is perhaps one of the most delicate aspects of navigating anniversaries and birthdays. It's essential to allow space for both mourning and celebration, acknowledging the pain of loss while also embracing the joy that your child brought into your life. This balance does not negate the significance of your loss but rather honors the full spectrum of your relationship with your child. It acknowledges that grief and joy can coexist, giving the other depth. On these days, allow yourself to reflect on the happy memories and the love shared, even as you acknowledge the sadness that their absence brings. This approach fosters healing and enriches your child's legacy, ensuring that their memory is celebrated with the same richness and complexity with which they lived their life.

As this chapter closes, we reflect on the importance of rituals and remembrance in the grief journey. Whether through personalized memorials, private rituals, or the creation of new traditions on significant dates, these practices serve as vital tools for honoring your child's legacy and navigating the complex emotions of grief. They provide tangible ways to connect with your child's memory, allowing for expressions of love and sorrow and fostering a sense of continuity and hope. As we move forward, we carry these memories and traditions with us, weaving them into the fabric of our lives and our hearts, ensuring that the love we hold for those we have lost continues to inspire and guide us.

Chapter 3: The Impact on Personal Identity and Family Dynamics

---

The Transformation of Sarah's Family

Sarah's world shattered the day her son, Daniel, died in a tragic accident. As she stood by his graveside, her heart felt like it was breaking into pieces she could never hope to gather. Her identity, so long tied to being Daniel's mother, seemed to vanish in the cold wind that swept through the cemetery. She asked herself, "Who am I now? How do I continue without him?"

In the weeks following Daniel's death, Sarah found herself lost in a haze of grief. The roles that had once defined her—caregiver, mentor, protector—felt hollow. She struggled to engage with the world, feeling disconnected from everything she had once loved. Her husband, James, and daughter, Emily, were grappling with their own sorrow, and the family dynamic shifted in ways they hadn't anticipated.

James became withdrawn, throwing himself into his work to escape the pain. Emily, on the other hand, was vocal about her grief, seeking comfort in her friends and sometimes lashing out in anger. Once filled with laughter and the sounds of daily life, the house was now a silent battleground of unspoken emotions and misunderstood intentions.

One evening, as the family sat in the living room, Emily broke the silence. "We need to talk about Daniel," she said, trembling but determined. "Pretending we're okay isn't helping anyone."

Her words were a catalyst. The family began sharing their memories of Daniel—his mischievous grin, love for music, dreams, and ambitions. They cried together, but for the first time in months, they also laughed, remembering the joy he had brought into their lives.

This shared grief became a bridge, helping them navigate the painful terrain of their new reality. They honored Daniel's memory by creating a scholarship fund, supporting aspiring musicians like him. This project gave them a collective purpose, a way to channel their grief into something meaningful.

Sarah found solace in volunteering at a local grief support group, where she met other parents who had lost children. These connections were a lifeline, helping her understand that her feelings were valid and that finding a new sense of self was possible. She began to see her identity not as diminished but as transformed by her experiences. She was still Daniel's mother but was also a survivor, an advocate, and a source of strength for others.

James, too, began to heal. He started attending therapy, where he learned to express his emotions and reconnect with his family. He and Sarah grew closer, their shared pain forging a deeper bond. Emily channeled her grief into her studies, inspired by her brother's passion for learning, and she became an advocate for mental health awareness at her school.

Through their journey of grief, Sarah and her family discovered that their identities were not fixed but fluid, capable of evolving in response to the deepest losses. They learned that while Daniel's absence would always be felt, his presence would continue to shape their lives profoundly and positively. The family, once shattered, began to rebuild, finding strength in their shared love and memories.

When the unimaginable happens—the loss of an adult child—you not only confront the profound sadness of your grief but also face a seismic shift in your own identity. The reflection in the mirror may seem unchanged, yet you might feel that an essential part of your being has altered irrevocably. This chapter delves into the transformative journey of self-redefinition that follows the loss of a child, exploring how this pivotal event reshapes your sense of self and impacts family dynamics and how, through the depths of grief, unexpected pathways to personal growth can emerge.

Who Am I Now? The Parent's Grief Identity

Identity Shifts in Grief

In the wake of your child's passing, you may find yourself pondering deeply existential questions: "Who am I without my child?" and "How can I carry on?" Your role as a parent to your child was a significant part of your identity, and their absence may leave you feeling unsure about your role and purpose moving forward. This shift can affect every aspect of your life—from interacting with others to engaging with your passions. It's as if you must learn to navigate the world anew through a lens tinted with grief and longing. As challenging as this may seem, permitting yourself to explore these changes is essential. Acknowledging that your identity is evolving in response to your loss is crucial in adapting to your new reality. It allows you to begin redefining your sense of self, not as a departure from who you were but as an expansion, incorporating your past experiences and circumstances.

Navigating the New Normal

As you adjust to life without your child, the concept of a "new normal" often feels like a misnomer. How can anything feel normal when such a significant part of your life is now absent? Yet, this new normal is not about replacing old realities or forgetting past joys but about integrating your loss into your life and allowing it to reshape your existence in meaningful ways. This might mean adopting new routines that fit your current emotional landscape or reevaluating your priorities and responsibilities. Perhaps you find that activities that once brought joy have lost their luster, urging you to seek new sources of fulfillment. Or maybe you discover a heightened capacity for compassion and empathy, guiding you towards volunteering or advocacy work. Embracing these changes doesn't diminish your love for your child; instead, it honors their impact on your life by allowing their memory to influence your path.

Personal Growth Through Grief

Amidst the sorrow, a profound opportunity for personal growth often emerges. With its raw intensity, grief can strip life down to its bare essentials, clarifying what truly matters. This clarity can lead to reevaluating your values and priorities, perhaps catalyzing a newfound appreciation for the present moment or a deeper understanding of your emotional resilience. Engaging with this transformative aspect of grief requires courage and self-reflection. It might involve journaling your thoughts and feelings, seeking therapeutic guidance to navigate your emotional journey, or simply allowing yourself to feel and express your emotions fully. Through these actions, you can begin to weave your loss into the fabric of your being, not as a defining scar but as a part of a larger narrative of love, resilience, and growth.

Supporting Each Other's Grief Identity

Each member's grief journey is unique in a family, and recognizing and supporting these individual journeys is crucial for collective healing. Open, honest communication about feelings and experiences can help prevent misunderstandings and build mutual support. Family therapy or shared grief counseling sessions can provide a safe space to explore these emotions, facilitating a deeper understanding of each other's needs and expressions. Celebrating each person's milestones in their grief journey is also essential, recognizing that each step forward is a testament to the strength and love that binds your family together. By supporting one another in these ways, you can build a resilient family dynamic that honors your child's memory and supports each member's individual path to healing.

Navigating the reshaping of your identity and family dynamics post-loss is undoubtedly challenging. Yet, it is also a path filled with potential for profound personal growth and deeper familial bonds. By embracing these changes and supporting each other through the process, you and your family can find ways to continue honoring your loved one's legacy while forging paths enriched by memories and guided by love.

Supporting Siblings in Grief: A Delicate Balance

When a family faces the heartbreak of losing a child, each member's grief journey reflects their unique relationship with the lost loved one and their coping mechanisms. Siblings, often referred to as the "forgotten mourners," face a particularly complex grief process. They not only grapple with their profound loss but also witness the deep sorrow of their parents, which can profoundly affect their grieving process. Recognizing the distinct experience of each sibling is crucial. It's important to acknowledge that each sibling may display their grief differently—some might withdraw, seeking solitude. In contrast, others might express their pain more outwardly or even seem to move on more quickly. These variations are normal and reflect personal grief styles rather than the depth of their feelings. Parents can support each sibling by acknowledging their individual grief and providing opportunities to express their feelings safely and without judgment. This might involve facilitating one-on-one discussions where siblings can share their thoughts and emotions about the loss or providing them professional grief counseling, which can offer personalized strategies for processing their emotions.

Encouraging open and honest communication among siblings is crucial in maintaining their emotional health and family cohesion. Creating a family culture where open expression of feelings is normalized can help siblings feel safe to share their grief. Regular family meetings can be an excellent platform for this, providing a set time and space for each family member to talk about their feelings or share memories of their deceased sibling. During these meetings, it's helpful to remind siblings that all emotions are valid and that there's no right or wrong way to feel. This practice fosters understanding and support among siblings and strengthens their emotional connections to each other, providing a shared space for healing.

Creating spaces for individual grieving is equally essential. Just as siblings need collective family support, they also benefit from having personal space to grieve in their way. This might mean setting up individual areas in the home where they can retreat when they need solitude. Encouraging personal hobbies or activities that allow for emotional expression, such as art, music, or writing, can also provide therapeutic outlets for their feelings. Parents should be attentive to each sibling's needs for both private and shared grieving times, recognizing that the need for solitude does not necessarily mean a withdrawal from the family connection but rather a different approach to processing their grief.

Family activities that foster connection are essential in helping siblings and parents support each other through grief. Planning activities that the entire family can participate in, such as cooking a favorite meal of the deceased sibling, watching their favorite movie, or visiting places significant to them, can create new, positive memories that honor the loved one's life. These activities can be particularly beneficial on anniversaries or birthdays, turning days that might otherwise be solely painful into times of meaningful family connection and remembrance. Additionally, involving siblings in planning these activities can give them a sense of agency and purpose, helping them feel that they are actively contributing to the family's healing process.

Through these approaches, families can navigate the complex dynamics of sibling grief with compassion and understanding. By acknowledging each sibling's unique grief, fostering open communication, allowing for individual grieving spaces, and engaging in activities that strengthen family bonds, parents can support their children in adapting to life after loss while honoring the memory of the sibling they mourn. This delicate balance of collective and individual grieving is critical to building a supportive family environment where each member can find their path to healing.

Maintaining a Relationship with a Partner While Grieving

Navigating the emotional terrain of grief within a partnership can be profoundly challenging. The loss of a child is an immense ordeal that both partners endure, yet the way each person processes this grief can vary significantly. This divergence can lead to misunderstandings and feelings of isolation at a time when support from one another is most needed. Recognizing the complexities of grieving as a couple is the first step toward navigating this delicate aspect of your relationship. It's crucial to understand that while you share the loss, your emotional experiences and needs might differ. One partner may seek to express their feelings openly and discuss them less frequently. At the same time, others might prefer to grieve more privately or through action, such as immersing themselves in work or physical activities. These differences, which can be stark during such a vulnerable time, require patience and understanding. By acknowledging that there is no 'right' way to grieve, you can begin to navigate this shared yet individual experience with compassion and empathy.

Communication plays a pivotal role in maintaining a healthy relationship while grieving. It's essential to create an environment where open, honest dialogue about your feelings, fears, and needs is encouraged. Regular check-ins can be beneficial, where partners can express their current state of mind without fearing judgment. These conversations might not always be easy; they can stir intense emotions and sometimes lead to discomfort. However, the act of sharing your grief can bring a deeper understanding and intimacy. It's also helpful to verbalize appreciation for the support you receive from each other, recognizing that both of you are navigating a profoundly tricky situation. If communication becomes too challenging, seeking the help of a counselor or therapist skilled in grief counseling can provide a safe space to explore these feelings and learn effective communication strategies that respect both partners' grieving styles.

Respecting the differences in grieving styles is crucial for the health and stability of your relationship in the wake of such a loss. Giving each other space to grieve individually is essential for finding common ground. For instance, if one partner finds solace in solitude, providing them with time alone can be an act of love and understanding. Conversely, if the other derives comfort from talking about the deceased or participating in activities in their memory, finding ways to support these needs can show deep care and empathy. It's about balancing these needs without judgment, recognizing that each approach is valid and essential. This respect for individual needs helps prevent resentment or misunderstanding arising from the misalignment of grieving processes.

Finding ways to reconnect as a couple is essential amid grief. It can be easy to feel disconnected as each person deals with their sorrow, potentially leading to a drift in the relationship. To counter this, consider establishing new rituals or activities that you can do together to foster closeness and comfort. This might include regular walks in a place special to your child, cooking meals together, or participating in a hobby that offers a respite from grief. These activities don't need to revolve around the loss but should provide a space to enjoy each other's company and strengthen your bond. Additionally, rituals such as lighting a candle for your child during significant dates or creating a memory box together can serve as meaningful ways to connect in your shared love and memory of your child. These shared activities and rituals can be powerful in maintaining a sense of partnership and mutual support, helping to navigate the grieving process together.

Navigating grief as a couple requires compassion, patience, and a willingness to understand and adapt to each other's emotional needs. By fostering open communication, respecting individual grieving styles, and finding ways to reconnect, you can support each other through this heartrending time, strengthening your relationship in the face of profound loss. Through these shared efforts, the bond between you can become a resilient foundation from which both of you can draw strength and comfort as you navigate the complexities of grief together.

Extended Family and Friends: Roles and Reactions

When a family navigates the profound waters of grief following the loss of an adult child, the ripples extend beyond the immediate family to include extended relatives and friends. Each individual connected to your family may react differently, influenced by their relationship with the deceased and their personal beliefs about death and mourning. Some might offer immediate and constant support, while others may struggle to express their condolences, appearing distant or overly concerned. Understanding these varied reactions is crucial, as it helps you manage your expectations and interactions with them during a sensitive time. For many, this understanding begins with recognizing that there is no uniform way to grieve and, thus, no 'right' reaction to such a loss. This realization can foster a sense of patience and grace with those around you, even when their responses might not align with what you need or expect.

Guiding supportive interactions among extended family and friends starts with clear communication. It's helpful to be honest about the type of support that feels most beneficial. For some, practical help such as managing day-to-day tasks or preparing meals might be most welcome, while others may appreciate regular check-ins or a space to talk about their child. Articulating these needs can guide your loved ones in how they can best support you, preventing feelings of helplessness or frustration on both sides. This might involve direct conversations or, sometimes, enlisting a close family member or friend to communicate your needs to a broader circle. Additionally, consider the power of inclusive activities that allow friends and family to feel involved, such as organizing a memorial event or participating in charity work in memory of your loved one. These actions not only bring people together but also channel collective grief into meaningful action.

Setting healthy boundaries with extended family and friends is also paramount. Grief can leave individuals feeling vulnerable and exposed, making it essential to protect your emotional space. Setting boundaries might mean choosing not to attend certain gatherings, limiting conversations about your loss, or asking people not to share photos or memories on social media without your consent. It's important to communicate these boundaries kindly but firmly, ensuring that they are respected. Remember, setting boundaries is not an act of isolation but a necessary measure to preserve your well-being. It allows you to engage with others on your own terms, which can be crucial for managing grief.

Leveraging support from the wider community can also be a significant source of comfort and strength. This might involve reaching out to support groups in person and online, where you can connect with others who have experienced similar losses. Schools, workplaces, and faith communities can also be pivotal in providing a network of support. Engaging with these groups might include participating in counseling offered by schools or workplaces or attending grief support sessions organized by faith-based organizations. These resources often provide not only emotional support but also practical advice and solidarity in navigating the complexities of grief. Moreover, they can act as a bridge between personal suffering and communal support, highlighting that while your loss is profoundly personal, you are not alone in your journey of grief.

In navigating interactions with extended family, friends, and the broader community, maintaining a balance between personal needs and external support becomes key. By understanding varied reactions, guiding supportive interactions, setting clear boundaries, and leveraging community support, you can create a supportive network that respects your grief while offering the compassion and connection needed during this challenging time.

As we close this chapter on the dynamics of grief within extended relationships, we understand that each interaction, whether challenging or supportive, shapes our experience of loss and recovery. The insights gained here pave the way for our next discussions on deeper aspects of grief, guiding us through the transformative processes that follow losing a loved one.

Chapter 4: Seeking Professional Help and Community Support

The path through grief, layered with its complex emotions and unexpected turns, often requires more than personal resolve and the support of friends and family. It demands a kind of professionally informed and deeply empathetic guidance. Recognizing when you need this level of support is not a concession of weakness but a courageous acknowledgment of your situation's unique challenges. This chapter is designed to help you navigate the intricate process of finding the right therapist, one who not only understands the depths of grieving a lost child but also facilitates a nurturing space where healing can begin to take root.

A Story of Seeking Professional Help and Community Support

When Mark lost his adult son, Jacob, in a sudden accident, his world was irrevocably shattered. Jacob had been his confidant, his fishing buddy, and his greatest source of pride. The thought of continuing life without him seemed impossible. In the weeks following Jacob's death, Mark found himself struggling to get out of bed, his days blurring into a haze of grief and despair.

Friends and family did their best to support him, offering words of comfort and a listening ear, but Mark felt an overwhelming sense of isolation. The pain was too deep and personal for anyone else to truly understand. His wife, Linda, watched helplessly as Mark withdrew further into himself, his silence a stark contrast to the vibrant man she had known for decades.

One day, Linda gently suggested that Mark consider talking to a professional. At first, he resisted. Sharing his innermost thoughts with a stranger felt foreign and uncomfortable. But as the weight of his grief grew heavier, Mark realized he needed more support than his loved ones could provide.

Mark began his search for a therapist by reflecting on his specific needs. He recognized that his grief was multifaceted, laced with anger, guilt, and an overwhelming sense of loss. He wanted someone who could help him navigate these complex emotions and offer strategies to manage his overwhelming sorrow.

After identifying what he needed, Mark looked for a therapist who specialized in grief counseling. He read reviews, asked for recommendations from friends, and contacted local support groups. Eventually, he found Dr. Harris, a therapist with years of experience in helping individuals cope with profound loss.

From their first session, Mark felt a sense of relief. Dr. Harris provided a safe, non-judgmental space where he could express his emotions freely. She helped him understand his feelings were valid and part of the grieving process. With her guidance, Mark began to explore his grief, confronting the anger and guilt that had been consuming him.

Dr. Harris introduced Mark to coping strategies, such as mindfulness exercises and journaling, which helped him process his emotions and find moments of peace amidst the turmoil. She encouraged him to engage in activities that once brought him joy, even if they now seemed tinged with sorrow. Slowly, Mark started to reclaim small pieces of his life, honoring Jacob's memory while allowing himself to heal.

In addition to therapy, Mark found solace in joining a support group for parents who had lost adult children. Initially hesitant, he discovered a community of individuals who truly understood his pain. Sharing his story and hearing others' experiences helped Mark feel less alone in his grief. The support group became a lifeline, offering empathy, understanding, and a sense of camaraderie.

Through the combined efforts of professional therapy and community support, Mark began to navigate his path through grief. He learned that healing did not mean forgetting Jacob but finding a way to live with the loss. Dr. Harris and his support group helped him see that his grief was a testament to the love he had for his son and that by embracing his pain, he could also embrace the joy and memories Jacob had brought into his life.

Mark's journey through grief was not linear. There were days when the pain felt as raw as the moment he first heard the news. But with the right support, he discovered the strength to face each day, honoring his son's legacy while finding a new way forward.

As you read this chapter, remember that seeking professional help and community support is a brave and vital step in your journey through grief. It is a recognition that your loss is profound and that healing, while difficult, is possible with the right guidance and understanding.

The path through grief, layered with its complex emotions and unexpected turns, often requires more than personal resolve and the support of friends and family. It demands a kind of professionally informed and deeply empathetic guidance. Recognizing when you need this level of support is not a concession of weakness but a courageous acknowledgment of your situation's unique challenges. This chapter is designed to help you navigate the intricate process of finding the right therapist, one who not only understands the depths of grieving a lost child but also facilitates a nurturing space where healing can begin to take root.

4.1 Finding the Right Therapist: Tips and Red Flags

Identifying Your Needs

Before embarking on the search for a therapist, it's crucial to understand what you need from them. Grief is not a uniform experience; it varies wildly from one person to another, influenced by individual personalities, the nature of the loss, previous experiences with grief, and existing support systems. Start by reflecting on what aspects of your grief feel most unmanageable. Are you struggling with overwhelming emotions, such as anger or guilt? Do you find it challenging to engage in everyday activities, or are you withdrawing from relationships? Perhaps you're grappling with existential questions that the loss of your child has precipitated. Understanding your specific needs will help you articulate what you're looking for in a therapist, whether someone who offers cognitive-behavioral strategies, specializes in grief, or provides a more spiritually oriented-approach to healing.

Searching for a Therapist

Finding a therapist experienced in grief counseling and with whom you feel comfortable can significantly impact your healing process. Start by asking for referrals from healthcare providers, friends, or family members who have undergone similar experiences and may know a therapist with relevant expertise. Professional organizations and therapy networks also offer directories of licensed practitioners specializing in grief and bereavement. When reviewing potential therapists, consider their educational background, certifications, and the approaches they use. It's often helpful to arrange an initial consultation, which many therapists offer at no cost. This meeting can be an opportunity to ask about their experience with grief, their therapeutic approach, and any other questions that might help you gauge whether they could fit your needs.

Recognizing Red Flags

While most therapists are well-intentioned, not all will suit your unique needs. Recognizing red flags during initial consultations or the first few sessions is essential. Be wary of therapists who promise quick fixes to your grief or who seem to impose their agendas or beliefs about what your grieving process should look like. A therapist who minimizes your feelings or pushes you to make decisions or 'move on' before you're ready can also impede your healing. Another red flag is a lack of empathy or disconnection during sessions, making you feel unheard or unsupported. Trust your instincts; therapy is deeply personal, and feeling safe and understood is crucial.

The Therapeutic Relationship

The relationship you build with your therapist is foundational to effective grief therapy. This relationship, often termed the 'therapeutic alliance,' is built on trust, mutual respect, and collaboration. A good therapist listens without judgment, validates your feelings, and helps you explore them quickly. They should offer empathy and understanding, provide insights that resonate with your experiences, and encourage your agency in the healing process. As therapy progresses, this relationship can become a transformative space where you not only work through the pain of your loss but also discover new ways to connect with the memory of your child and envision a future where joy and sorrow can coexist.

Reflection Section

Consider journaling about what you hope to achieve through therapy. Reflect on your challenges and the changes you wish to see in handling grief. This exercise can clarify your goals for therapy, making it easier to communicate your needs to a potential therapist and evaluate your progress once therapy begins.

Navigating the search for a therapist while you're grieving requires energy and resolve, but finding the proper support can be a pivotal step in your healing journey. As you move forward, remember you are not alone in this search. Many have walked this path before you, and with the proper support, you can find your way through the intricate landscape of grief toward a place of renewed hope and meaning.

4.2 Support Groups: Shared Grief and Understanding

When you're grappling with the loss of your adult child, the feeling of isolation can be profound. In these times, finding a community that shares your experience can be a lifeline. Support groups bring together individuals who, despite their diverse backgrounds, share the common thread of loss, creating a unique space where collective understanding and empathy flourish. The benefits of joining such a group are manifold. Initially, you might find solace simply in the presence of others who understand the depth of your grief without needing you to explain or justify your feelings. Over time, these groups can also become a valuable resource for sharing strategies that help manage the day-to-day challenges of living with grief. Participants often share resources such as books, therapies, and personal coping strategies, enriching their toolkit for handling grief. Moreover, seeing others at various stages of their grieving process can provide hope and a sense of perspective that might be difficult to find elsewhere.

Finding the right support group requires careful consideration to ensure it aligns with your needs and comfort level. Start by identifying what type of group might best suit your situation. Some groups are structured with a focus on specific types of loss, such as the loss of an adult child, while others may be more general. Consider also the facilitation style of the group; some are led by professional therapists or counselors who can provide skilled guidance, while peer-led groups offer shared experiences in a less formal setting. To find these groups, you can ask for recommendations from healthcare providers or community centers or search online databases specializing in grief support resources. Visiting a group at least once before committing can also give you a sense of whether its style and the dynamics of its members feel supportive and comfortable for you.

The choice between online and in-person support groups is another consideration, as each format offers distinct advantages and challenges. In-person groups foster a sense of immediate community and connection, allowing for physical expressions of support, such as hugs or a comforting presence, that can be very powerful. However, they might require commuting and may not be available in all areas, potentially limiting accessibility. Online groups, on the other hand, offer the convenience of accessing support from your home and connecting with a broader geographical range of participants, which can be particularly helpful if your specific type of loss feels isolated or uncommon in your immediate area. The drawback, however, is that the virtual format can sometimes feel less personal, and the nuances of communication, such as tone of voice or body language, are often lost in digital interactions.

Setting realistic expectations for participation in a support group is crucial for a positive experience. It's important to understand that support groups are not a replacement for therapy but rather a complementary form of support. The benefits vary widely among individuals; some may find immediate comfort and long-term connections, while others might find it takes several meetings to start feeling the benefits. Regular attendance is often crucial to developing a sense of belonging and efficacy. It's also vital to recognize that discussions can sometimes be triggered as members share their own stories and emotions. Preparing yourself to face potentially complex topics that may resonate closely with your experiences is integral to the process.

In these shared spaces, the power of collective experience can become a tool for healing and understanding. As you listen to others and share your journey, the path of grief can feel less lonely and more part of a shared human experience. The support and insights gained from these groups can be invaluable in navigating your grief, providing comfort and understanding when both can be hard to find.

4.3 Online Communities:

Connection in the Digital Age

In the vast expanse of the internet, amidst myriad connections and networks, lie communities that gather individuals bound by similar threads of experience, particularly those navigating the waves of grief. Engaging with online grief communities can offer a unique form of solace and understanding, providing a platform where emotions and stories are shared across global boundaries, making the world feel smaller and less isolating. When seeking such online spaces, it is vital to approach them with a sense of purpose and awareness. Start by identifying platforms that resonate with your specific type of grief. There are numerous forums, social media groups, and websites dedicated to grief and specific types of loss, such as the loss of an adult child. Websites like GriefNet.org and The Compassionate Friends offer structured environments moderated by professionals. At the same time, social media platforms like Facebook and Reddit host various grief-related groups that are more peer-driven.

Once you find a potentially supportive community, observe the interactions before fully engaging. This can give you insight into the community's norms, the types of support offered, and whether the tone and interaction style align with what you find comforting. When you decide to engage, remember that the anonymity of online interactions can sometimes lead to misunderstandings due to the lack of non-verbal cues. Communicating clearly and interpreting others' responses with generosity is helpful. Engaging authentically, sharing your story, and responding to others can foster connections and provide mutual support that transcends physical distances.

Maintaining privacy and safety while participating in online forums or social media groups is paramount. It is easy to overlook how much personal information we share in these spaces. Start by carefully reviewing the privacy settings on any platform you use, ensuring your personal information is protected, and you have control over who can view your posts. Be cautious about sharing details that could compromise your security or your family. Additionally, consider creating boundaries around how much and what parts of your grief you share. While being open can lead to meaningful exchanges, preserving your emotional safety is essential by not sharing aspects of your experience that feel too raw or private.

The value of shared stories in online grief communities cannot be overstated. Reading and hearing about others' experiences with loss can validate your feelings and help you understand that your reactions are normal and that you are not alone in your struggle. These stories can also be educational, providing insights into coping mechanisms that might not have occurred to you. They can offer hope, showing paths to adjustment and adaptation that others have found. In sharing your own story, you not only contribute to this tapestry of collective wisdom but might also find a sense of purpose and catharsis in expressing your journey, helping to process your grief in ways that face-to-face conversations sometimes cannot accommodate.

However, the limitations of online support are essential to recognize. Virtual connections, while valuable, cannot wholly replicate the nuanced support that face-to-face interactions can provide. The lack of physical presence and the inherent delays in communication can sometimes lead to feelings of disconnectedness or misinterpretation. Additionally, the sheer volume of shared grief stories, while often comforting, can occasionally feel overwhelming or triggering. It's crucial to monitor how your engagement with these communities affects your emotional state and to step back when necessary. If you find that online interactions no longer serve your needs, or if your grief feels too complex and persistent, it might indicate the need for more structured, professional support beyond these communities. In such cases, turning to a grief counselor or therapist who can offer personalized guidance might be the next step in your healing process.

Navigating the world of online grief communities offers a blend of anonymity and intimacy, allowing you to connect with others who understand your loss while maintaining control over your engagement level. As you explore these digital spaces, let them supplement but not replace the rich, multifaceted support system that face-to-face interactions, professional counseling, and personal reflection provide. In doing so, you harness the collective power of shared experiences, weaving them into your tapestry of grief and recovery and finding, in the stories of others, the echoes of your resilience and hope.

4.4 When to Seek Help: Recognizing the Signs of Complicated Grief

In the landscape of loss, where emotions ebb and flow with often unpredictable intensity, a form of grief lingers, resisting the passing of time. This is known as complicated grief, a condition where the natural process of grieving is stalled, trapping individuals in a persistent state of sorrow that disrupts their ability to function in daily life. Understanding complicated grief involves recognizing that while grief itself is a normal response to loss, complicated grief is characterized by its extended duration and the severity of its symptoms, which remain acute long after the loss has occurred. It differs from typical grief reactions that, despite their intensity, gradually lead to an acceptance of loss and a re-adjustment to life. Complicated grief, on the other hand, feels as though time stands still, with sufferers reliving their loss without the emotional abatement that typically occurs as days turn into months.

Identifying when additional help is needed is crucial for anyone struggling with complicated grief. The signs can be subtle or overt, but they commonly include an intense longing for the deceased that does not decrease with time, pervasive sadness or depression, a sense of meaninglessness about life, and a withdrawal from social activities that were once enjoyable. Other indicators might include anger or bitterness over the loss, difficulty trusting others since the loss, and an inability to enjoy life or think about the future. It might be time to seek professional help if these feelings sound familiar. The persistent nature of these symptoms often means that coping strategies that typically help with normal grief may not be practical, necessitating specialized intervention to move forward.

Encouraging those experiencing these symptoms to seek professional help is essential to healing. This might involve consulting with a healthcare provider who can assess the symptoms and possibly refer you to a mental health professional specializing in grief counseling. Treatment for complicated grief may include therapies that focus on trauma and loss, helping individuals to process their grief and begin to envision a future where they can remember their loved ones without the intense pain currently felt. Therapeutic approaches can vary, but they often involve helping the individual to confront avoided situations or painful memories, re-establish relationships with others, and find personal significance and meaning in life after loss.

Supporting a loved one who is experiencing complicated grief requires patience, understanding, and a proactive approach. It's important to encourage open conversations about their feelings, allowing them to express their sorrow without fear of judgment. Regularly check in on them, offering support for daily tasks or accompanying them to therapy sessions if they are open to it. Be mindful of the language around recovery, avoiding phrases suggesting they should move on or get over their loss. Instead, focus on affirming their feelings, supporting their healing at their own pace, and encouraging them to seek professional help if the symptoms of grief become overwhelming or debilitating. In doing so, you provide a compassionate space that acknowledges their pain while guiding them toward avenues for professional help that can offer hope and healing.

This chapter explores the nuanced realm of seeking professional help and community support in the face of profound grief. From understanding when it's time to seek professional intervention for complicated grief to navigating the waters of support groups and online communities, the journey through grief often requires a multifaceted approach. As you move forward, remember the importance of recognizing the signs that additional support is needed, whether for yourself or a loved one, and taking the steps to seek that support. By doing so, you honor both the depth of your loss and the possibility of recovery, moving towards a future informed by love and memory but not overshadowed by pain.

As we close this chapter, we transition from understanding the external supports available in navigating grief to turning inward and exploring personal resilience and growth in the next chapter. Here, we will delve into how personal practices, self-care, and renewed purpose can form the building blocks of a life that continues to honor loved ones lost while embracing the potential for joy and fulfillment in the coming days.

Chapter 5: The Diverse Stages of Grief

When you face the profound loss of an adult child, you find yourself walking through the twilight of your old life into the uncertainty of a new existence shaped by grief. This transformative period is marked by pain, profound learning, and personal growth, which unfold in various stages. Each stage, with its unique challenges and revelations, offers vital insights into your psyche and provides a framework for understanding your journey through grief.

A Story of Denial and Isolation

When Maria received the phone call informing her that her daughter, Lisa, had been in a fatal car accident, the world seemed to stop. The words echoed in her mind, but their meaning felt distant and unreal. Lisa, her vibrant and loving daughter, couldn't be gone. This had to be a mistake. In the days following the news, Maria found herself in a state of denial, a cocoon that shielded her from the unbearable reality.

She continued to set a place for Lisa at the dinner table, half expecting her to walk through the door with her usual bright smile. Maria's husband,

Tom, tried to talk to her about making arrangements for the funeral, but she couldn't bring herself to engage in the conversations. She found solace in isolation, retreating to Lisa's room, surrounded by her daughter's belongings as if being close to them could bring her back.

Maria's friends and family reached out, offering condolences and support, but she pushed them away. It was easier to pretend that Lisa was away on a trip, that her phone would ring any moment, and that she would hear her daughter's voice again. The protective veil of denial kept the full force of her grief at bay, allowing her to function, albeit in a daze.

Tom, worried about Maria's detachment, gently suggested that they see a grief counselor together. At first, Maria resisted the idea, unwilling to confront the pain she was so desperately trying to avoid. But as the days turned into weeks, the cracks in her denial began to show. She found it increasingly difficult to maintain the illusion that Lisa would return. The weight of reality started to seep in, bringing with it a flood of emotions that were impossible to ignore.

In their first session with the grief counselor, Maria hesitated to open up. But as the counselor, Dr. Patel guided them through their feelings, Maria began to understand that her denial was a natural, albeit temporary, defense mechanism. Dr. Patel explained that facing the reality of Lisa's death was a necessary step toward healing and that it was okay to move through this process at her own pace.

Dr. Patel encouraged Maria to share her memories of Lisa and talk about the beautiful moments they had shared. Slowly, Maria started to open up, tears flowing as she recounted stories of Lisa's laughter, kindness, and dreams. The process was painful, but it also brought relief, as if speaking about Lisa allowed her spirit to remain present in a different way.

Maria realized that her isolation prevented her from finding the support she needed. She began to allow her friends and family back into her life, accepting their offers of help and their shared memories of Lisa. She understood that her grief, while deeply personal, was also shared by those who loved Lisa.

As the protective veil of denial continued to lift, Maria faced the raw pain of her loss. It was overwhelming at times, but she learned that by acknowledging her grief, she could begin to navigate it. She started to engage in activities that honored Lisa's memory, such as volunteering at the animal shelter where Lisa had spent so much of her time. These acts of remembrance brought comfort and a sense of pain, helping Maria to slowly rebuild her life around the absence of her daughter.

Through Dr. Patel's guidance and her loved ones' support, Maria discovered that moving through denial was not about forgetting Lisa but about finding a new way to live with her memory. It was a step toward healing, allowing her to embrace the reality of her loss while holding onto the love that would always remain.

As you read this chapter, remember that denial and isolation are natural parts of the grieving process. It is important to allow yourself the time and space to move through these stages at your own pace. With the right support and understanding, you can begin to face the reality of your loss and find a path toward healing.

As the sun sets, casting long shadows that fade into twilight, it often heralds a period of reflection and quiet. Similarly, when you face the profound loss of an adult child, you find yourself walking through the twilight of your old life into the uncertainty of a new existence shaped by grief. This transformative period is marked by pain, profound learning, and personal growth, which unfold in various stages. Each stage, with its unique challenges and revelations, offers vital insights into your psyche and provides a framework for understanding your journey through grief.

5.1 Denial and Isolation: Facing Reality

Understanding Denial

In the initial aftermath of loss, denial acts as your psyche's first line of defense against an unbearable reality. It cushions the immediate shock, allowing you to process the initial pain in doses you can handle. This denial can manifest as disbelief—rejecting the fact that your child is genuinely gone, expecting them to walk through the door at any moment. This period is not about choosing ignorance but rather a subconscious protective mechanism that shields you from the full impact of your grief until you are more equipped to face it. Gradually, as the protective veil of denial begins to lift, the reality of the loss seeps in, and with it comes the flood of emotions that denial had held at bay. It's crucial during this time to gently remind yourself that moving through denial is a necessary step towards healing, and it's okay to take this step in your own time and in your own way.

Feeling Isolated

As you grapple with the denial and slow acceptance of your loss, you might also experience a profound sense of isolation. It may feel as though no one truly understands the depth of your pain or the complexity of your emotions. This isolation can be exacerbated by well-meaning friends or family who, unsure of how to help, might give you space that you interpret as neglect. Combating this isolation involves reaching out for connection, even when it is difficult. This can be through sharing your feelings with trusted friends, joining a support group, or participating in community activities that align with your interests. These connections remind you that although your grief journey is unique, you are not alone in your experience of loss.

Gradual Acceptance

Navigating through denial and isolation eventually leads you toward acceptance, but it's important to understand that this acceptance is not about being okay with the loss. Rather, it's about acknowledging the reality of the loss and understanding that it is a permanent part of your life story. This acceptance is gradual and often non-linear, marked by moments of progress and regression periods. It involves integrating the loss into your life narrative, learning to live with it, and allowing it to reshape your understanding of the world and yourself. Patience with yourself during this time is crucial; just as wounds of the body take time to heal, so do wounds of the heart.

Leaning on support systems is critical to help mitigate feelings of isolation and assist you in the gradual move toward acceptance. These systems can include family, friends, therapists, or support groups—anyone who provides emotional or practical support. They act as pillars that you can lean on when the weight of your grief feels too heavy to bear alone. These support networks allow you to share your burden, making it more manageable and providing a sense of shared humanity and understanding. These connections often light the way through the darkness of grief, guiding you toward a place of greater peace and acceptance.

In this stage of your grief, as you oscillate between denial, isolation, and gradual acceptance, remember that each step, no matter how small, is a part of your journey toward healing. These experiences, while challenging, are also opportunities for profound personal growth and understanding. They allow you to explore the depths of your emotions, understand your needs and limits, and discover the resilience within you that sustains you through your darkest times and guides you toward light and renewal.

5.2 Anger: Channeling and Understanding Its Power

In the vast landscape of grief, anger often emerges as a visceral, powerful emotion that can feel overwhelming and terrifying. It's a natural response to the profound sense of injustice and powerlessness that accompanies the loss of an adult child. Anger can manifest in various ways, from a simmering irritation to a fierce rage that can shock even those who feel it. Recognizing this anger as a normal part of grief is crucial; it validates your feelings and allows you to address them without self-judgment. Anger in grief is not a sign of weakness nor a moral failing. Instead, it's a profound expression of love, loss, and the disruption of life's natural order. Your anger underscores the depth of your bond with your child, highlighting the pain of their absence in your life.

Finding healthy outlets for this anger is essential. Physical activities can be particularly effective, as they allow you to channel your emotional energy into physical exertion. Activities like running, boxing, or even more gentle options like yoga, not only help in releasing the build-up of anger but also stimulate the production of endorphins, natural mood lifters. These activities provide a double benefit: they help manage the immediate intensity of your anger and improve your overall well-being. Creative expression is another therapeutic outlet. Painting, writing, making music, or engaging in any form of art can transform your raw emotions into something tangible, often providing new insights into your feelings. Art offers a voice to your anger, allowing it to be heard and acknowledged in a form that can be both personal and universally understood.

The emotions fueling your anger in grief are often complex and rooted in feelings of helplessness, fear, or guilt. Helplessness might come from the recognition that you could not prevent your child's death; fear might be tied to the uncertainty of living without them; guilt might stem from wondering if there was something more you could have done. These feelings are intricately tied to your love for your child and your inherent desire to protect them, making them difficult to express or fully acknowledge. Addressing these underlying emotions is a critical part of processing your anger. This might involve talking through your feelings with a therapist or a trusted friend, writing about them, or reflecting on them during meditation. Understanding these roots can diminish the power of anger over time, turning it into a signal of deep-seated emotions that need attention rather than an overwhelming force.

Finally, forgiveness and release play a pivotal role in managing anger. Forgiveness here does not necessarily mean absolving others or yourself from real or perceived mistakes. Instead, it's about softening the harshness of self-judgment and releasing the grip of anger about things you cannot change. This part of healing is perhaps one of the hardest but most liberating. It involves acknowledging that anger, while understandable, often holds you bound to the very pain you wish to heal from. Releasing this anger through forgiveness can be a profound step towards peace. It does not mean forgetting or diminishing the significance of your loss but rather allowing yourself to remember and grieve without the additional burden of anger. This release might not happen all at once, and that's perfectly normal. It's a process that can unfold in small steps, each taking you closer to a place of greater peace and acceptance.

5.3 Bargaining: The What Ifs and If Onlys

In the depths of grief, it is not uncommon to find yourself caught in bargaining, a stage where the mind seeks to negotiate its way out of pain, often through a maze of "what if" and "if only" scenarios. This bargaining is essentially a manifestation of our deep-seated desire to regain control over something that feels utterly uncontrollable—the loss of a loved one. As you wrestle with the finality of death, your mind might race with thoughts like, "What if I had called them that night?" or "If only I had insisted they go to the doctor sooner." These thoughts are attempts to rewrite history, to find a way that the outcome could have been different, reflecting a yearning not just for your loved one's return but also for the return of a world that once felt safe and predictable.

Dealing with these feelings of regret and the persistent thoughts of bargaining can be one of the more tortuous aspects of grieving, as they tether you to an unchangeable past and often intensify the pain. One effective strategy to manage these thoughts is acknowledging their presence openly without judgment. Please recognize that these thoughts are a normal part of the grieving process; they do not signify weakness or irrationality. Writing these thoughts down can sometimes help externalize them, providing a clearer perspective on their unrealistic nature and allowing you to challenge their validity. Another approach is to talk through these feelings with someone who understands—perhaps a therapist or a support group member—who can offer both empathy and objectivity, helping you to see that these thoughts, while average, are not rooted in reality but rather in an understandable desperation to undo the unchangeable.

Moving beyond the bargaining stage involves a gradual shift of focus from the past to the present, from what cannot be changed to what can still be influenced—your healing. This shift is crucial as it involves accepting the reality of the loss, thereby allowing yourself to engage with your grief rather than trying to negotiate it away. It's about letting go of the illusion of control over the past and embracing the possibility of influence over your future emotional landscape. Redirecting your energy towards activities that promote healing can facilitate this shift. Engaging in meaningful activities, whether reconnecting with nature, rediscovering old hobbies, or dedicating time to projects your loved one would have cared about, can all be part of regaining a sense of agency often lost in the bargaining phase.

Mindfulness practices play a pivotal role in this transition by fostering a state of presence that anchors you in the current moment, reducing the frequency and intensity of bargaining thoughts. Techniques such as focused breathing, meditation, or gentle yoga help cultivate an awareness of the present, teaching you to observe your thoughts and feelings without attachment. This mindful presence encourages a compassionate acceptance of your emotional state, reducing the distress caused by thoughts of what might have been. By regularly practicing mindfulness, you can develop a greater capacity to withstand and process the pain of loss, gradually finding within yourself the strength to accept the unchangeable and cherish the memories of your loved one without the painful overlay of regret and guilt.

Through these strategies, the bargaining stage of grief, with its painful regrets and relentless what-ifs, can be navigated with compassion and understanding. By directly acknowledging and addressing the thoughts of bargaining, shifting your focus towards healing, and practicing mindfulness, you can begin to loosen the grip of these thoughts on your heart and mind, paving the way for a more peaceful acceptance and a renewed engagement with life in the present moment. This stage, challenging though it may be, is yet another step in the journey of grief that, while it cannot bring back what was lost, can lead to a deeper understanding of yourself and your capacity to heal and to continue loving in the face of loss.

5.4 Depression: Navigating the Depths

In the shadowed valleys of grief, where the light of joy seems dim and distant, depression can often be a silent companion. It's crucial to distinguish between profound sadness—a natural response to your tremendous loss—and clinical depression, which can engulf all aspects of your life and persist far beyond the initial mourning period. Profound sadness is marked by moments of relief where memories bring smiles, not just tears, and where support from loved ones can temporarily lift the spirits. Clinical depression, however, colors all experiences with a persistent hue of hopelessness and exhaustion, often requiring more than just time and comfort to heal. It can manifest as a pervasive feeling of emptiness, a lack of pleasure in almost all activities, significant weight changes, or a constant fatigue that sleep does not relieve. Understanding these distinctions is vital because each requires different approaches and interventions.

Self-care during periods of intense sadness or depression is not about indulgence but about survival and recovery. Tailoring self-care practices to address the symptoms of depression during grief specifically is essential. This might include setting a routine that fosters small accomplishments, significantly boosting mood and motivation. Simple activities like making your bed, preparing a meal, or walking can provide a sense of control and normalcy. Nutrition plays a critical role in managing depression. Foods rich in omega-3 fatty acids, such as fish, walnuts, and flaxseeds, and those high in folate, such as leafy greens and legumes, can help ease depressive symptoms. Moreover, staying connected to a support network, even when you feel like withdrawing, can provide a lifeline during deep despair. Regular check-ins with friends or family, attending grief counseling or support groups or just having a coffee with a friend can all be part of a regime that helps pierce the isolation that often accompanies depression.

Given the severity and persistence of depressive symptoms, it is often necessary to seek professional support. There's a strength, not a weakness, in recognizing when your coping strategies need reinforcement from therapeutic interventions or medical treatment. A mental health professional can offer therapies such as cognitive-behavioral therapy (CBT), which has been effective in treating depression by helping to change negative thought patterns and behaviors. In some cases, medication may be recommended as part of your treatment plan. Antidepressants can correct chemical imbalances affecting your mood, though they should be carefully managed under the guidance of a healthcare provider to find the right type and dosage.

Amidst the struggles with depression and grief, connecting with others who understand your pain can be a beacon of hope. Stories of resilience and recovery—shared in support groups or through counseling—can offer comfort and models for navigating your dark times. Hearing how others have faced similar emotions and found paths through them can inspire steps you might take in your healing process.

These stories underscore that while your journey is unique, you are not alone in your struggle. They remind you that recovery is not only possible but also a realistic expectation, offering a glimmer of hope when the path ahead seems enveloped in shadows.

As you navigate the profound depths of depression during your grief, remember that this, too, is a part of your process—challenging yet crucial to traverse. By understanding the nature of your sadness, implementing strategic self-care practices, seeking necessary professional help, and finding solace in the stories of others, you can start to reclaim pieces of a life reshaped by loss. This chapter does not close the book on your experience of depression but opens the door to strategies and support that can lead you towards a slowly brightening future.

In reflecting on the diverse stages of grief explored in this chapter—from the initial shock and denial to the depths of depression—we see a landscape filled with challenges but also with pathways that can lead us through. Each stage's unique experiences and emotions contribute to our healing process. As we turn the page to the next chapter, we carry with us the understanding and strategies gleaned here, ready to explore how personal resilience and renewed purpose can further shape our journey of grief and recovery.

The first moments after receiving the heartbreaking news are often marked by an intense emotional whirlwind. You might find yourself in a state of shock, disbelief, or numbness, unable to grasp the reality of what has occurred. This numbness, often the mind's temporary shield against intense pain, can be confusing and disorienting. It's important to understand that these reactions are natural protective responses of the human psyche trying to cope with acute emotional distress. They do not signify a lack of feeling but rather an overwhelming influx of emotion that your mind is trying to process. During these initial hours, giving yourself permitting discussing your feelings, reminiscing about your child, or simply sitting together in silence, the presence of someone who cares can help mitigate the experience of these feelings without judgment, which is crucial to your emotional well-being.

Make a Difference with Your Review

People who give without expectation live longer, happier lives and make more money. So if we've got a shot at that during our time together, darn it, I'm gonna try.

Unlock the Power of Generosity

People who give without expectation live longer, happier lives and make more money. So if we've got a shot at that during our time together, darn it, I'm gonna try.

To make that happen, I have a question for you...

Would you help someone you've never met, even if you never got credit for it?

Who is this person you ask? They are like you. Or, at least, like you used to be. Less experienced, wanting to make a difference, and needing help, but unsure where to look.

Our mission is to make [how to survive the death of an adult child] accessible to everyone. Everything I do stems from that mission. And, the only way for ME to accomplish that mission is by reaching…well...everyone.

This is where you come in. Most people judge a book by its cover (and its reviews). So here's my ask on behalf of a struggling parent in mourning you've never met:

Please help that the first moments after receiving the heartbreaking news are often marked by an intense emotional whirlwind. You might find yourself in a state of shock, disbelief, or numbness, unable to grasp the reality of what has occurred. This numbness, often the mind's temporary shield against intense pain, can be confusing and disorienting. It's important to understand that these reactions are natural protective responses of the human psyche trying to cope with acute emotional distress. They do not signify a lack of feeling but rather an overwhelming influx of emotion that your mind is trying to process. During these initial hours, giving yourself permitting discussing your feelings, reminiscing about your child, or simply sitting together in silence, the presence of someone who cares can help mitigate the experience of these feelings without judgment, which is crucial to your emotional well-being. by leaving this book a review.

Your gift costs no money and takes less than 60 seconds to make real, but it can change a fellow parent in mourning life forever. Your review could help…

...one more entrepreneur support their family.

...one more employee get meaningful work.

..one more client transform their life.

...one more dream come true.

To get that 'feel good' feeling and help this person for real, all you have to do is...and it takes less than 60 seconds...

leave a review.

Simply scan the QR code below or click on the link to leave your review:

https://www.amazon.com/review/create-review/?ie=UTF8&channel=glance-detail&asin=B0D5KT5B2X

If you feel good about helping a faceless parent who has lost their adult child, you are my kind of person. Welcome to the club. You're one of us.

I'm much more excited to help you ACHIEVE TARGET OUTCOMES than you can imagine. You'll love the STRATEGIES I will share in the coming chapters.

Thank you from the bottom of my heart. Now, back to our regularly scheduled programming.

- Your biggest fan,

G.M.Grace

PS - If you provide something of value to another person, it makes you more valuable to them. If you'd like goodwill straight from another parent who has lost an adult child - and you believe this book will help them - send this book their way.

Chapter 6: Finding New Meaning and Purpose

A Story of Redefining Purpose After Loss

When Tom lost his adult daughter, Megan, to a sudden illness, he felt his world collapse. Megan had been his rock, his source of joy and inspiration. The void left by her absence was profound and all-encompassing. In the following weeks and months, Tom struggled to find his footing in a life that now felt unfamiliar and hollow.

Tom found himself questioning his identity and purpose. Who was he without Megan to share his daily life with? How could he find meaning in a world that seemed to have lost its color? These questions haunted him, casting long shadows over his days.

One day, while sifting through Megan's belongings, Tom came across her journal. In it, she had written extensively about her dreams and passions, her love for the environment, and her desire to make a difference in the world. Inspired by her words, Tom decided to honor her legacy by volunteering at a local environmental conservation group.

Initially, the work was challenging. Each visit to the park, where they planted trees and cleaned up trails, reminded him of the walks he used to take with Megan. But as he continued, Tom found solace in the work. It felt like a way to stay connected to Megan, to keep her spirit alive through actions that reflected her values and passions.

Gradually, Tom began to redefine his purpose. He took on a leadership role within the conservation group, organizing events and raising awareness about environmental issues. The work provided a new sense of fulfillment and connection, turning his grief into a force for positive change.

Tom also started attending support groups for bereaved parents, where he found a community of individuals who understood his pain. Sharing his journey with others who had experienced similar losses helped him feel less isolated. He found strength in their stories and, over time, began to offer support and guidance to new group members.

The journey of grief, while deeply personal, often brings us to a crossroads where the past and the future intersect in the present moment. Here, amidst the memories and echoes of what was, you may contemplate a daunting and uncharted future. It is in these quiet reflections that the seeds of new meaning and purpose can be planted. As you navigate this delicate terrain, embracing your child's legacy can illuminate pathways once shadowed by sorrow, guiding you toward a life enriched with new passions and pursuits.

6.1 Redefining Purpose After Loss

Identity and Purpose

The loss of a child is a profound upheaval that reverberates through every aspect of your life, raising fundamental questions about your identity and purpose. Who are you now that your child's physical presence is no longer a part of your daily life? How do you find purpose when a significant part of your world has shifted? These questions, while daunting, are also gates to deeper self-understanding. Redefining your identity and purpose post-loss does not mean leaving behind the bond you shared with your child. Instead, it involves weaving your child's love, lessons, and memories into the new dimensions of yourself and your life's purpose. This might mean adopting new roles or returning to aspects of your identity that were overshadowed by your focus on being a parent. It could also involve channeling your experiences into helping others navigate similar paths, transforming your pain into empathetic action. This redefinition is not a process that occurs overnight but is a gradual unfolding, where each step reflects who you were and who you are becoming.

Legacy of Love

Consider how your child's unique qualities and passions can inspire a renewed sense of purpose. Did they have particular causes they cared about or hobbies they loved? Incorporating these elements into your life keeps your connection to your child vibrant and can guide you to new pursuits that bring fulfillment and joy. For example, if your child was passionate about environmental conservation, you might find purpose in volunteering for or supporting initiatives that protect natural habitats. Each action taken in their memory can be a stepping stone towards a legacy of love—a testament to your child's impact on your life and the world.

Small Steps

The path to finding and embracing new aspects of your identity and purpose is best navigated in small, manageable steps. Start by setting simple, achievable goals that encourage you to engage with the world around you. This might be as straightforward as joining a book club, taking a class in something you've always been interested in, or setting aside time each week to explore a new hobby. These activities are not just about filling time; they are stepping stones that can lead you to new passions and connections, helping to rebuild a sense of engagement and joy in life. Each small step is a thread in the new tapestry of your life, colored by memories of the past but woven into new experiences and discoveries.

Support in Exploration

As you venture into new territories of self and purpose, the support of friends, family, and community can be invaluable. Sharing your goals and interests with supportive others can open opportunities for connection and exploration that you might not have considered. Additionally, joining in-person or online groups that share your emerging interests can provide encouragement and camaraderie as you explore new parts of yourself. For those who find themselves struggling to take these steps alone, seeking the guidance of a counselor or therapist can provide the support needed to move forward. These professionals can offer understanding validation and practical strategies for coping with the fear and uncertainty often accompanying this part of your journey. They can help you to see this time of exploration not as a departure from who you were but as an expansion of who you are—enriched by the love and memories of your child and empowered by new experiences and connections.

In redefining your purpose after loss, remember that each new interest or activity you pursue carries with it a thread of your love for your child, woven into the ongoing narrative of your life. These pursuits are not about moving on from your grief but about moving forward with it, carrying the love and legacy of your child into each new day and each new experience. As you take these steps, you honor not only the memory of your child but also your capacity for resilience and renewal—qualities that define the profound journey of healing and hope.

6.2 Creating a Legacy in Honor of Your Child

Creating a lasting legacy for a child who has passed away is a profound way of honoring their life and the impact of those around them. One meaningful approach is through memorial projects, which can take various forms depending on what resonates most with the family and the community. For instance, creating a community garden or playground can be a vibrant tribute, offering a place of joy and reflection for you and the entire community. Such spaces provide a growing and evolving living memory, much like your child's memory in the hearts of those who loved them. Another impactful project could be an art installation in a public space that reflects aspects of your child's life or passions. This could be a mural in a local park or a sculpture in a community center, providing a visual expression of their spirit and a focal point for communal remembrance and storytelling.

The impact of these memorials extends beyond the immediate family, touching the lives of community members and often becoming a part of the communal landscape. They transform personal loss into shared spaces of comfort and remembrance, strengthening community bonds and fostering a sense of collective healing. Furthermore, these projects often encourage community involvement and collaboration, which can be immensely therapeutic. They keep your child's memory alive and ensure that their legacy continues to inspire and engage others in positive ways.

In addition to physical memorials, setting up scholarships or foundations can be a powerful way to extend your child's influence into the future. If your child has a particular passion or a cause they care about, such as environmental conservation, animal welfare, or the arts, establishing a scholarship to support others in pursuing these interests can be incredibly impactful. The practical steps to setting this up typically involve deciding on the criteria for the scholarship, such as the field of study, the level of education (high school, undergraduate, postgraduate), and any specific qualifications candidates must meet. Partnering with an educational institution or a scholarship administration service is also important to manage the funds and selection process. Foundations, similarly, can fund projects, research, or initiatives that align with your child's interests or values. These require more management and oversight but can have a broad impact, supporting causes your child cared about on a larger scale.

Personal storytelling is a profound aspect of creating a legacy. Sharing stories about your child's life, the lessons they taught you, the joys you shared, and even the challenges you faced together helps keep their memory alive in a very personal way. These stories, shared in various formats, can provide comfort and a sense of understanding, weaving a rich tapestry of memories that celebrate their life from multiple perspectives and helping others to feel connected to your child's enduring legacy.

Through these endeavors—whether they are in creating physical spaces that invite communal interaction, establishing scholarships or foundations that propel your child's passions into the future, or sharing personal stories that underscore their lasting impact—you do more than just preserve memories. You build an enduring legacy that mirrors your child's love, passions, and values, ensuring their influence continues to resonate within and beyond your community. This legacy, crafted with love and sustained through communal and personal remembrance, is a testament to a cherished life and a presence deeply missed yet forever influential.

6.3 Volunteering: Giving Back as a Healing Mechanism

Volunteering after the loss of an adult child can be transformative. It opens a channel through which your grief finds a purpose, transforming the deep reservoirs of sorrow into springs of healing and solidarity. Engaging in service provides a distraction from the pain, a profound connection to the community, and a sense of purpose that might feel lost in the wake of such a significant personal tragedy. This transformative power of volunteering can empower you and offer a glimmer of hope in your healing process.

Finding volunteer opportunities that resonate with your passions or honor your child's interests can be particularly meaningful. If your child loved animals, consider volunteering at a local animal shelter where caring for animals in need can provide comfort and joy. If they were passionate about literacy or education, you might consider tutoring students or organizing book drives. These activities keep your child's spirit alive in your daily actions and create a legacy of kindness and generosity that mirrors their values and passions. When selecting a volunteer opportunity, consider what makes you feel connected to your child and what might provide a meaningful outlet for your grief. This alignment of personal interests and giving back can significantly enhance the therapeutic benefits of volunteering, making it a powerful tool in your healing process.

Moreover, the act of helping others can itself be a source of healing. Engaging in volunteer work puts you in touch with individuals who, although they may be facing different challenges, are also experiencing their forms of suffering and recovery. This can lead to a deep sense of solidarity and mutual support. For instance, participating in community-building projects like constructing community gardens or homes for those in need can create spaces of collective effort and shared purpose, where personal losses and triumphs blend into the more extensive human experience of resilience and hope. These interactions can remind you that sorrow and joy coexist, often leading to profound personal insights and emotional breakthroughs that might not have surfaced in isolation.

When considering volunteer work, assessing your readiness and ensuring that the commitment aligns with your current emotional and physical capacity is important. Volunteering should not become a source of stress or a means of avoiding your grief. Choosing engagements that respect your current state and offer flexibility is crucial. Start with short-term commitments and consider roles that allow you to control the pace and intensity of your involvement. This could mean choosing activities that can be done at home or ones that occur in group settings where responsibilities can be shared. Furthermore, ensure that the organization you choose to volunteer for understands your situation and supports your needs as someone navigating a significant loss. This understanding can substantially affect how rewarding and healing the volunteer experience is.

Through volunteering, you can redefine parts of your world that the loss of your child has altered. Each act of service, each connection made through volunteering, adds layers of meaning and purpose to your life that can help mend the fragmented parts of yourself, guiding you toward a path where grief and growth coexist, each informing the other in profound ways. This path, marked by giving and receiving, creates a bridge between your personal experiences and the communal tapestry of human endeavor, showing that even in loss, the potential for renewal and connection exists.

6.4 Embracing New Hobbies and Interests

Exploring new hobbies and interests can be a profound way to weave joy and meaning back into the fabric of your life after the loss of your child. This exploration is not just about filling time; it's about rediscovering who you are in the wake of your loss and what resonates with the new person you are becoming. Engaging in new activities can reignite a sense of curiosity and passion that grief may have dulled. It's about allowing yourself to try new things without expectations and finding joy in the process rather than solely in the outcomes. Whether learning to paint, joining a dance class, or starting a garden, each new hobby offers a window into different aspects of your personality and interests, some of which you might not have been aware of before your loss.

The therapeutic benefits of creative outlets like art, music, or writing are particularly profound. These activities provide a means to express feelings that might be too complex or overwhelming to articulate in words. For instance, painting or sculpting can translate the depth of your grief into visual expressions, providing a release that might be hard to achieve through conversation. Similarly, music can resonate with your emotions on a primal level, offering comfort and a sense of connection to shared human experiences of loss and recovery. Writing, whether keeping a journal, crafting poems, or composing letters to your child, helps in processing feelings and can be a significant step toward healing. These creative expressions help manage grief and construct a new self-identity that integrates your experiences and emotions in a meaningful way.

Physical activity is another vital area supporting physical and emotional healing. Activities like hiking, yoga, or swimming improve physical health and help regulate the emotional highs and lows that accompany grief. The rhythmic nature of physical activities provides a meditative experience, a respite from the churn of tumultuous emotions. Moreover, the endorphins released during exercise naturally enhance your mood and outlook. Physical activities can also reconnect you with your body, helping you understand and appreciate its needs and capabilities, which might have been neglected during intense periods of mourning.

Connecting with others who share your interests can further enrich the experience of exploring new hobbies. Joining clubs or groups that align with your new interests provides social support and helps build a community that understands and shares your passion. Whether it's a book club, a gardening group, or a cycling team, these social connections can offer encouragement and motivation to continue exploring and enjoying new activities. They also provide a sense of normalcy and belonging, crucial to rebuilding your life after loss. Engaging with these communities allows you to form new friendships and strengthen existing ones, weaving an invaluable support network in times of need.

As you allow yourself to engage in new hobbies and interests, remember that each step forward is a testament to your resilience and capacity to find joy and meaning in life again. These activities are not just hobbies; they are gateways to healing, self-discovery, and reconnection with the world around you. They offer a way to honor your journey, celebrate your child's life, and embrace the future with renewed purpose and joy.

This chapter explored how engaging in new hobbies and finding creative and physical outlets can significantly aid healing. These activities provide a diversion from grief and a means to rebuild and redefine oneself in the aftermath of profound loss. As we close this chapter, we carry forward the understanding that each new activity and connection forms a part of the more extensive journey of recovery—a journey marked by both challenges and triumphs, each step taken a reflection of the enduring love for the child we remember and honor. As we transition into the next chapter, we will delve deeper into the spiritual aspects of healing, exploring how spiritual beliefs and practices can provide comfort and understanding in the journey through grief.

Chapter 7: The Role of Spirituality and Belief

A Story of Spirituality vs. Religion: Finding Comfort in Beliefs

When Elizabeth lost her adult son, Daniel, in a tragic accident, her grief felt insurmountable. She had always been spiritual, attending church regularly and finding comfort in her faith. However, Daniel's sudden death shook her beliefs to their core. She grappled with questions that her religious doctrines couldn't easily answer.

In the initial weeks after Daniel's passing, Elizabeth sought solace in her church community. The familiar rituals and prayers provided a temporary refuge, a semblance of normalcy in a world turned upside down. Yet, as time passed, she felt a growing disconnect between her grief and the answers her religion offered. The assurances of an afterlife and divine plan felt hollow in the face of her profound loss.

Desperate for understanding, Elizabeth began to explore spirituality beyond the confines of her traditional beliefs. She started reading books on various spiritual traditions, from Buddhism to Native American spirituality, seeking perspectives that resonated with her experience of loss. Through this journey, she discovered practices like mindfulness meditation and nature walks, which brought her a sense of peace and connection that she hadn't felt in months.

One evening, as Elizabeth sat quietly in her garden, she felt an overwhelming sense of Daniel's presence. The gentle rustling of leaves and the soft chirping of birds seemed to speak to her of her son. A profound, comforting moment transcended her previous understanding of spirituality. She realized that her connection with Daniel could exist in many forms beyond the dogmas of her religion.

Elizabeth began incorporating these new spiritual practices into her daily life. She meditated each morning, reflecting on her love and memories with Daniel. She joined a local support group that encouraged spiritual exploration, where she met others who had experienced similar losses and were on their journeys to finding meaning and comfort.

*Through these experiences, Elizabeth found
that spirituality and religion did not have to be
mutually exclusive. Enriched by new spiritual
insights, her faith became a more flexible,
compassionate support system. She learned to hold
space for her grief, finding solace in both the rituals
of her church and the broader spiritual practices she
had embraced.*

*Elizabeth's journey through grief taught her
that finding comfort in beliefs is a deeply personal
process. It's about creating a spiritual tapestry that
reflects your unique experiences, blending old
traditions with new practices to support and heal you.
Her story is a testament to the power of spiritual
exploration, showing that comfort and understanding
can be found in the most unexpected places.*

Personal Beliefs: A Source of Solace and Understanding

Your personal beliefs, whether rooted in formal religion or a more individual sense of spirituality, can be an essential anchor during profound loss. These beliefs often provide a framework that helps make sense of the seemingly senseless, offering perspectives on suffering, the nature of life and death, and the possibility of an afterlife or continued existence beyond the physical. For many, these beliefs are abstract concepts and real, palpable sources of comfort. They can offer assurances of reunion with lost loved ones or affirmations of a more excellent plan, which, even in the depths of grief, can provide a kind of solace that is both profound and healing. Engaging with these beliefs through prayer, meditation, or quiet contemplation can help stabilize the tumultuous emotions of grief, providing moments of peace and clarity amidst the chaos.

Exploring Spirituality: Beyond Traditional Frameworks

While some find solace within the established rituals and beliefs of their religion, others may feel a calling to venture into spirituality in a broader, more diverse manner. This exploration can be profoundly enriching, especially if traditional religious beliefs do not fully encompass the complexities of your grief or if they clash with your personal experiences of loss. Exploring spirituality might involve delving into various spiritual traditions, practicing mindfulness or yoga, or simply immersing oneself in nature, feeling a connection to something greater. This journey is a personal odyssey that can lead to the discovery of a spiritual path that resonates more with your inner experiences and needs. It's a process of crafting a spiritual identity that can cradle and uplift your grief, providing a framework that echoes your truths and experiences.

Respecting Diverse Beliefs: Embracing Spiritual Plurality

In your exploration of spirituality, you may encounter various beliefs and practices, each with its insights and wisdom on the nature of life, death, and mourning. Respecting this diversity is crucial, not only as a principle of tolerance but also as a way of enriching your spiritual journey. Engaging with beliefs that differ from yours can expand your understanding of how humans cope with loss, highlighting the universalities and particularities of grief across cultures and spiritual traditions. This engagement can be as simple as reading about other faiths, attending interfaith dialogues, or participating in the rituals of other traditions with an open heart and mind. Embracing a plurality of spiritual expressions can deepen your empathy and broaden your perspective, enriching your spirituality with a tapestry of human experience and wisdom.

Finding Community: The Support of Spiritual Fellowship

For many, the most profound aspect of spirituality is the community it fosters. Whether centered around a specific religion or more eclectic, spiritual communities can offer vital support and a sense of belonging in the aftermath of loss. These communities provide a space for shared rituals and beliefs, communal understanding, and empathy. Participating in community services, prayer meetings, meditation groups, or spiritual study can connect you with others who share your beliefs and grief, offering comfort and solidarity. In these spaces, you can share your pain and your journey and also listen to the experiences of others, creating mutual support grounded in a shared spiritual perspective. This fellowship can be incredibly sustaining, providing a buffer against the isolation of grief and a source of hope and collective healing.

In spirituality and belief, you find a landscape rich with diversity and depth, offering paths that can lead to comfort, understanding, and connection. Whether refining old beliefs, exploring new spiritual territories, or engaging with a community of shared faith, your spiritual journey can be vital to your healing process, providing anchors of peace and beacons of light in the often-turbulent sea of grief. As you explore these paths, remember that your journey is uniquely yours—shaped by your beliefs, loss, and hopes. It is a testament to your love for your child and the resilience of the human spirit in the face of profound loss.

This story and accompanying discussion highlight the importance of finding comfort in spirituality and beliefs during the grieving process. Each person's journey is unique, and the exploration of spirituality can provide profound insights and healing.

7.1 Spirituality vs. Religion: Finding Comfort in Beliefs

In the quiet, reflective moments of your grief, you might find yourself searching for solace in realms beyond the tangible—turning towards spirituality or religion to find comfort and understanding in your loss. The quest for spiritual solace can be as diverse as the individuals seeking it, each weaving their unique tapestry of belief and longing against the backdrop of their grief. Whether you find yourself reaffirming old beliefs, questioning long-held doctrines, or exploring new spiritual landscapes, this journey can be a profound source of comfort, insight, and even transformation.

Personal Beliefs: A Source of Solace and Understanding

Your personal beliefs, whether rooted in formal religion or a more individual sense of spirituality, can be an essential anchor during profound loss. These beliefs often provide a framework that helps make sense of the seemingly senseless, offering perspectives on suffering, the nature of life and death, and the possibility of an afterlife or continued existence beyond the physical. For many, these beliefs are abstract concepts and real, palpable sources of comfort. They can offer assurances of reunion with lost loved ones or affirmations of a more excellent plan, which, even in the depths of grief, can provide a kind of solace that is both profound and healing. Engaging with these beliefs through prayer, meditation, or quiet contemplation can help stabilize the tumultuous emotions of grief, providing moments of peace and clarity amidst the chaos.

Exploring Spirituality: Beyond Traditional Frameworks

While some find comfort within their religion's established rituals and beliefs, others might feel compelled to explore spirituality in a broader, more eclectic way. This exploration can be significant if traditional religious beliefs do not fully address the nuances of your grief or if they clash with your personal experiences of loss. Exploring spirituality might involve reading widely from different spiritual traditions, engaging in practices like mindfulness or yoga, or simply spending time in nature, feeling a connection to something larger than oneself. This journey is deeply personal and can lead to discovering a spiritual path that aligns more with your inner experiences and needs. It's a process of building a spiritual identity that can hold and support your grief, providing a framework that resonates with your truths and experiences.

Respecting Diverse Beliefs: Embracing Spiritual Plurality

In your exploration of spirituality, you may encounter various beliefs and practices, each with its insights and wisdom on the nature of life, death, and mourning. Respecting this diversity is crucial, not only as a principle of tolerance but also as a way of enriching your spiritual journey. Engaging with beliefs that differ from yours can expand your understanding of how humans cope with loss, highlighting the universalities and particularities of grief across cultures and spiritual traditions. This engagement can be as simple as reading about other faiths, attending interfaith dialogues, or participating in the rituals of other traditions with an open heart and mind. Embracing a plurality of spiritual expressions can deepen your empathy and broaden your perspective, enriching your spirituality with a tapestry of human experience and wisdom.

Finding Community: The Support of Spiritual Fellowship

For many, the most profound aspect of spirituality is the community it fosters. Whether centered around a specific religion or more eclectic, spiritual communities can offer vital support and a sense of belonging in the aftermath of loss. These communities provide a space for shared rituals and beliefs, communal understanding, and empathy. Participating in community services, prayer meetings, meditation groups, or spiritual study can connect you with others who share your beliefs and grief, offering comfort and solidarity. In these spaces, you can share your pain and your journey and also listen to the experiences of others, creating mutual support grounded in a shared spiritual perspective. This fellowship can be incredibly sustaining, providing a buffer against the isolation of grief and a source of hope and collective healing.

In spirituality and belief, you find a landscape rich with diversity and depth, offering paths that can lead to comfort, understanding, and connection. Whether refining old beliefs, exploring new spiritual territories, or engaging with a community of shared faith, your spiritual journey can be vital to your healing process, providing anchors of peace and beacons of light in the often-turbulent sea of grief. As you explore these paths, remember that your journey is uniquely yours—shaped by your beliefs, loss, and hopes. It is a testament to your love for your child and the resilience of the human spirit in the face of profound loss.

7.2 Navigating Anger with God or the Universe

In the throes of grief, it is not uncommon to find yourself grappling with feelings of anger directed towards a higher power or the universe, particularly if you hold spiritual or religious beliefs. This anger can stem from a sense of betrayal, injustice, or abandonment, questioning why such a profound loss was allowed to happen. Recognizing and validating this anger is crucial—it is a natural response to the deep wounds inflicted by grief. It does not signify a loss of faith or a failure in spiritual strength; instead, it reflects the depth of your love and the pain of your loss. Addressing this spiritual anger involves acknowledging it openly, without self-judgment or guilt. It is essential to allow yourself to feel and express these emotions, understanding that they are part of the complex tapestry of grief.

Reconciling your faith with your experience of loss can be one of the most challenging aspects of navigating spiritual anger. You may oscillate between clinging to your beliefs and feeling utterly disconnected. This dissonance can be distressing but also represents an opportunity for deeper exploration and understanding of your faith. One approach is to reflect on the nature of your beliefs and how they interpret suffering and loss. Many spiritual traditions offer perspectives on suffering that can provide comfort and context, understanding it as part of a larger, often incomprehensible plan or as a catalyst for spiritual growth and deeper understanding. These teachings can sometimes offer a sense of peace and a framework to place your loss within a broader spiritual narrative.

Seeking spiritual counseling or guidance can be particularly beneficial when you are struggling to navigate the complex emotions related to your faith and loss. Spiritual leaders, counselors, or therapists specializing in grief can offer insights that resonate with your spiritual framework, helping you explore your feelings in a safe and supportive environment. They can facilitate discussions that delve into the nature of your anger, offering strategies to manage and integrate these feelings into your spiritual journey. This guidance can be invaluable in helping you reconstruct a sense of spiritual well-being that honors both your faith and your experience of loss.

Encouraging personal reflection and journaling can also be powerful tools for exploring and expressing your spiritual doubts and feelings. Journaling offers a private space to confront and clarify your emotions without fear of judgment. It allows you to document your thoughts and feelings, track changes and revelations, and reflect on your spiritual journey through grief. You might find it helpful to write letters to the higher power you believe in, expressing your anger, confusion, and questions. This act can be a form of catharsis, releasing intense emotions and helping you to find clarity and peace. Additionally, setting aside regular times for meditation or prayer can facilitate deeper introspection and connection with your spiritual beliefs, helping to soothe and heal the spiritual turmoil caused by your loss.

Navigating spiritual anger is a deeply personal journey that requires patience, openness, and compassion towards yourself. It's an ongoing dialogue between your beliefs and emotions, which can gradually lead to a renewed sense of faith and spiritual peace. As you continue to explore and reconcile these aspects of your grief, remember that there is no right or wrong way to traverse it. Each step, each realization, is a unique part of your path toward healing—a path marked by challenges and moments of profound insight and connection.

7.3 Signs and Messages: Interpreting Our Child's Presence

In the tender moments of solitude that often accompany the journey through grief, many find themselves sensing the presence of their lost loved ones in ways that transcend ordinary explanation. These experiences, often called spiritual signs, can manifest in myriad forms: a sudden breeze with no wind, a song that plays at the right moment, or even a recurring symbol that appears in unexpected places. These moments can feel like messages from your child, comforting and profound, suggesting that the bonds of love are not severed by death but transformed into a different kind of connection. For many, interpreting these signs provides comfort and a powerful affirmation of their ongoing relationship with their child.

The interpretation of such signs is profoundly personal and varies significantly from one individual to another. What might be a clear message to one person may appear as a mere coincidence to another. This variance underscores the importance of personal interpretation in recognizing and understanding these signs. If you find yourself experiencing events that you feel could be signs from your child, consider keeping a journal where you can note each occurrence along with your feelings and reactions. This practice not only helps in validating your experiences but also assists in discerning patterns or messages that may not be immediately obvious. Over time, this record can become a source of comfort and insight, offering tangible evidence of your child's continued presence in your life.

However, it's not uncommon to grapple with skepticism alongside a belief in signs from the beyond. You might find yourself oscillating between comfort in the sense that your child is still with you in some form, and doubt, questioning the reality of these experiences. This skepticism is a natural part of the grieving process, reflecting the internal conflict between the desire to hold on to your child and the need to accept their physical absence. Balancing these feelings can be challenging, but it is also a testament to the complexity of grief. Allowing space for both belief and skepticism can lead to a deeper understanding of your feelings and a more nuanced approach to spiritual signs. It's okay to question and analyze these experiences; doing so doesn't diminish their potential significance or the comfort they may bring. Rather, it can strengthen your emotional resilience, helping you navigate your grief with an open heart and mind.

Creating personal rituals to acknowledge and welcome these signs can also be a meaningful way to enhance your connection with your child. These rituals might include lighting a candle at a specific time, visiting a place special to your child, or simply setting aside a few moments each day to speak aloud to them. Engaging in these actions can create a structured space to express your grief and love, making the intangible connections feel more real and present. Moreover, these rituals can evolve into significant traditions that honor your child's memory and affirm your ongoing relationship with them. As you incorporate these practices into your daily life, they can provide comfort and a sense of continuity that helps bridge the gap between past and present, between the physical and the spiritual.

Interpreting signs from those who have passed is a journey of personal discovery and emotional exploration. Whether you find solace in these signs or face them with skepticism, their power lies in their ability to evoke reflection, provoke emotion, and encourage a deeper engagement with your feelings. As you navigate this complex terrain, remember that your experiences are valid, and your feelings are real. Embracing the possibility of ongoing connections with your child can be a comforting and transformative aspect of your journey through grief, providing not only solace but also a profound sense of love and continuity.

7.4 The Role of Faith Communities in Grief Support

In the tapestry of communal life, faith communities hold distinctive threads that can offer color and comfort, particularly through the intricate and often daunting grief process. These communities, rooted in shared beliefs and collective rituals, provide a unique form of support that can be a vital resource during the hardest times of your life. When you lose a child, the communal aspects of faith—shared prayers, congregational gatherings, and communal mourning—can offer a powerful sense of belonging and understanding, helping to buffer the intense feelings of isolation that often accompany profound loss.

Community Support: A Haven of Understanding and Empathy

Faith communities are more than just a gathering of individuals; they are a collective where shared beliefs and common experiences forge a deep sense of connection and mutual support. This communal aspect can be particularly comforting when you are grieving. Being part of a faith community provides a structured support system that understands the spiritual dimensions of grief. You might find solace in these communities' rituals and ceremonies, which often provide a space to honor your grief and commemorate your child within a framework of familiar and comforting rites. Moreover, the regular gatherings—weekly services or other community meetings—offer consistent touchpoints that can bring stability and routine when your world feels unmoored.

Grief and Faith Programs: Structured Support for the Bereaved

Many faith communities recognize the profound impact of loss and offer specific programs designed to support the bereaved. These might include grief counseling sessions led by clergy or trained volunteers, support groups that meet regularly to share experiences and coping strategies, or retreats that offer a chance for deeper reflection and healing in a supportive environment. These programs often combine spiritual teachings with practical, emotional support, helping you navigate your grief as a psychological journey and a spiritual passage. Engaging with these programs can also connect you with others experiencing similar losses, allowing you to build new relationships grounded in mutual understanding and shared recovery paths.

Interfaith Understanding: Broadening the Scope of Support

In an increasingly interconnected world, the opportunity to engage in interfaith dialogue and support groups can be particularly enriching for those navigating grief. These platforms offer a chance to explore how different faiths understand and manage grief, providing broader perspectives that might offer new insights or comfort. Interfaith groups encourage open dialogue and mutual support among people from diverse religious backgrounds, fostering an environment of inclusivity and shared human experience. Participating in such groups can broaden your spiritual perspectives and provide a deeper sense of global community, which can be particularly comforting when your personal grief journey feels isolating.

Respecting Boundaries: Navigating Personal and Communal Spaces

While faith communities offer significant support, navigating personal boundaries within these settings is crucial. Everyone's grief journey is unique, and what provides comfort to one person might not resonate with another. Communicating your needs and boundaries clearly to your community leaders and fellow members is important. For example, you might find certain rituals or discussions too painful or prefer private reflection over communal mourning. A respectful faith community will understand and accommodate these needs, ensuring that your engagement with communal support is helpful and not overwhelming. Moreover, setting these boundaries can empower you to engage with your faith community on your terms, making it a source of comfort rather than a place of stress.

In this exploration of the role of faith communities in providing support during grief, we see how these communities can offer unique and powerful forms of solace and connection. From structured support programs to the comfort of shared rituals and the broadening perspectives of interfaith dialogue, engaging with a faith community can provide a multifaceted support system that helps you navigate the complex emotions and spiritual questions that arise in the wake of losing a child. As you lean on this support, remember that your individual journey through grief is personal, and engaging with community resources should always respect and reflect your needs and boundaries.

Chapter 8: Transforming Grief into Action

A profound transformation can begin in the quiet aftermath of loss, where the echoes of a loved one's laughter once filled rooms are now hushed. For many who have walked through the valley of the shadow of grief, there comes a pivotal moment—a turning point where the acute pain of loss begins to morph into a force for change and advocacy. This chapter explores how the deep well of grief can be channeled into powerful advocacy and awareness campaigns that not only honor the memory of your loved one but also forge paths that lead others toward understanding and support. Here, you will discover how your journey through sorrow can unexpectedly position you as a beacon of hope and change for others.

8.1 Advocacy and Awareness: Making a Difference

A Story of Turning Pain into Advocacy

When Sarah lost her son, Mark, to a tragic accident caused by a drunk driver, she found herself engulfed in a whirlwind of grief and anger. Mark was a vibrant young man with a passion for life and a promising future. *The senselessness of his death left Sarah in a state of profound despair, but amidst her sorrow, a seed of determination began to grow.*

In the quiet moments of reflection, Sarah realized she needed to do something meaningful to honor Mark's memory. She started researching the impact of drunk driving and discovered that she was not alone in her experience. Countless families had suffered similar losses, and many had transformed their grief into powerful advocacy for change. Inspired by their stories, Sarah decided to channel her pain into action.

Sarah began by reaching out to local organizations dedicated to preventing drunk driving. She volunteered her time, sharing Mark's story at schools and community events to raise awareness about the devastating consequences of drunk driving. Her speeches were heartfelt and poignant, capturing the attention of those who listened and inspiring many to reconsider their choices.

Sarah's advocacy didn't stop there. She organized community events, such as walk-a-thons and candlelight vigils, to honor victims of drunk driving and to raise funds for educational programs. She also lobbied for stricter DUI laws, meeting with local lawmakers and using her story to illustrate the urgent need for change. Her efforts began to gain traction, and she found herself surrounded by a

---

Turning Pain into Advocacy

The journey from personal grief to public advocacy often begins in the quiet moments of remembrance, where the love and memories of your child inspire a desire to make a meaningful impact. Across the globe, countless parents have transformed their grief into action, advocating for causes that either resonate with their child or address the circumstances of their loss. For instance, parents who lost children to drunk driving accidents have become vocal advocates for stricter DUI laws. Others whose children struggle with mental health dedicate their efforts to dismantling the stigma surrounding mental illness and promoting greater access to mental health services. These stories of transformation illustrate the resilience of the human spirit and how personal loss can catalyze significant societal change. Engaging in advocacy offers a pathway to memorialize your child in a manner that reaches beyond personal memory into communal awareness and action.

Steps to Advocacy

Becoming involved in advocacy or awareness campaigns might seem daunting, but it can be approached through manageable steps. First, identify a cause that aligns closely with your experiences or your child's passions. Research organizations that are already working in this area and reach out to see how you can contribute. If you feel compelled to start your initiative, clearly define your goals and the message you want to convey. Building a network of support—connecting with other advocates, community leaders, and those who have walked similar paths—can provide invaluable resources and guidance. Social media platforms can also amplify your message and engage a broader audience. Remember, every small effort counts and contributes to the larger tapestry of change.

Community Engagement

The power of community engagement in advocacy cannot be overstressed. By involving your community, you broaden the impact of your efforts and promote a sense of collective healing and purpose. Organize community events, informational sessions, or workshops to raise awareness and educate others about the cause you are championing. Engaging local schools, community centers, and religious organizations can help disseminate your message more effectively. Community involvement turns individual advocacy into a collective movement, creating stronger momentum and fostering a supportive network to propel your cause forward.

Balancing Advocacy and Healing

While advocacy can be a healing experience, it's important to maintain a balance to ensure it does not become overwhelming. The emotional toll of revisiting personal loss through public advocacy can be significant, and it's crucial to recognize and honor your boundaries. Allow yourself time to rest and heal, stepping back when the emotional weight of advocacy feels too heavy. Integrating self-care practices into your routine can help maintain your well-being as you navigate the dual paths of advocacy and personal healing. Remember, true advocacy grows from a place of strength and healing, not from depleting your reserves.

In transforming your grief into action, you honor your child's memory and contribute to shaping a world that reflects the love and hope that their life represents. Through advocacy and awareness, your actions forge a legacy of change inspired by your deepest loss and propelled by your greatest love. As you engage with your community and advocate for meaningful causes, you embody the resilience and transformative power of love that continues to thrive, even in the face of profound sorrow.

8.2 Starting a Foundation or Scholarship in Your Child's Name

Creating a foundation or scholarship in memory of your child is a profound way to transform your grief into a lasting tribute that continues to positively impact the world. This process not only honors your child's spirit and legacy but also offers hope and support to others, extending the influence of your child's life beyond the confines of their physical presence. Establishing such a legacy requires thoughtful planning and a deep understanding of the goals you wish to achieve through this act of remembrance and generosity.

Legacy Foundations

The first step in creating a foundation or scholarship is to clarify your vision. What did your child care deeply about? Was there a specific cause they were passionate about, such as environmental conservation, education, or arts? Your foundation's mission should reflect these passions, continuing your child's values and interests. Once the mission is clear, the next step involves deciding the foundation's or scholarship's structure. Will it provide student scholarships, fund research, support community projects, or contribute to other causes? Determining the scope of the foundation's activities is crucial as it will guide all subsequent decisions.

For scholarships, define the criteria recipients must meet. Consider aspects such as academic fields, level of education (high school, undergraduate, postgraduate), specific achievements, or community involvement. These criteria should align with your child's interests or values, ensuring that the scholarship supports individuals who embody the spirit of what your child believed in or aspired to achieve.

Legal and Financial Considerations

Establishing a foundation or scholarship involves several legal and financial considerations that must be carefully managed to ensure the longevity and effectiveness of your efforts. You must register the foundation as a legal entity, typically a non-profit organization, which involves filing specific paperwork with state and federal agencies. This process might require a lawyer specializing in non-profit law to ensure compliance with all legal requirements.

Financial sustainability is another critical consideration. Initial funding might come from personal finances, fundraising events, or donations from family and friends. Setting up a clear financial plan that outlines the sources of funding, budgeting, and financial management practices. It may also be beneficial to establish an endowment, where a pool of money is invested, and only the income generated is used, ensuring the long-term sustainability of the scholarship or foundation.

Community Involvement

Engaging the community in your foundation's efforts is pivotal for its success and growth. Community support not only helps raise funds but also spreads awareness about the cause your foundation supports. Organizing fundraising events, such as charity runs, auction dinners, or concerts, can generate significant support and attention. Additionally, involving community members in the foundation's activities, such as selection committees for scholarships or volunteer projects, can foster a deeper community connection and investment in the foundation's goals.

Leveraging social media and online platforms can also play a crucial role in community engagement. These tools allow you to reach a broader audience, share your child's story and the foundation's mission, and garner support from beyond your local community. Regular updates, stories of impact, and transparent reporting on the foundation's activities can help build trust and ongoing support from a wide network of people.

Personal Stories of Impact

Sharing stories of how the foundation or scholarship has positively impacted others can be incredibly inspiring and affirming. For instance, you might share stories of scholarship recipients who have gone on to make significant contributions in their fields, embodying the spirit and values your child championed. Highlighting successful projects funded by the foundation that have benefitted communities can also illustrate the tangible impact of your efforts. These stories honor your child's memory and demonstrate the ongoing relevance and necessity of the foundation's work, encouraging continued support and engagement from the community.

In creating a foundation or scholarship in your child's name, you build a bridge between your love for your child and your desire to see their legacy continue to enrich and inspire the world. Through careful planning, legal and financial diligence, community engagement, and sharing impactful stories, your foundation or scholarship can stand as a lasting tribute to your child's life, making a meaningful difference in the lives of others and in the fabric of the community. This living legacy, crafted from your deepest loss and highest hopes, becomes a testament to the enduring power of love and the transformative potential of grief.

8.3 The Healing Power of Writing and Storytelling

In its many forms, writing serves as a powerful catharsis, offering a means to articulate the often-indescribable nuances of grief. For those who have lost an adult child, putting pen to paper or fingers to keyboard can be a profound way to process complex emotions and immortalize the memories of a beloved child. Whether through private journaling or public blogging, writing allows you to navigate the tumultuous waves of grief with a tool that is as fluid and expansive as the feelings it seeks to capture. Journaling privately offers a sanctuary where thoughts and emotions can be expressed without the constraints of external judgment. This practice can be particularly therapeutic; it's a space where you can pour out your heart, document your healing process, and observe the evolution of your grief without censorship. Writing helps externalize what is internal, providing clarity and insight that might not be evident when thoughts swirl tumultuously in your mind.

For those inclined to share their journey more publicly, blogging can be an equally therapeutic tool that connects you with others who may be walking similar paths. Sharing your story can dismantle the isolation that often accompanies grief, building bridges of empathy and understanding among those who read your words. However, the decision to share your grief journey publicly should be approached with consideration. Reflect on what you hope to achieve by sharing your story and prepare for a range of responses from readers. While many will offer support and empathy, there is potential for less sensitive reactions, which can be challenging to handle, especially in moments of vulnerability. Therefore, it's crucial to establish a strong support system and set emotional boundaries that protect your well-being when sharing your story in such a public way.

Participation in writing workshops or groups focused on grief and healing can further enrich the therapeutic experience of writing. These workshops provide a structured environment where guidance from experienced facilitators can help hone your writing skills, making your storytelling more impactful. More importantly, they offer a community of peers who understand the landscape of loss and can provide support, feedback, and encouragement. These settings often foster profound connections as participants share their writing and personal stories of love, loss, and healing. The collective experience of writing and sharing in a group can significantly diminish feelings of loneliness and misunderstanding, replacing them with a communal sense of acceptance and shared resilience.

Publishing your story can be meaningful for those considering a more formal presentation of their grief journey and memories. Whether you aim to reach others who are grieving, educate the broader public about the realities of loss, or simply create a lasting tribute to your child, publishing offers a way to share your story on a broader scale. However, navigating the world of publishing requires careful consideration. Assess your emotional readiness to share your story with a wide audience and consider the privacy of the loved and remembered. If you decide to pursue publication, various avenues are available, from traditional to self-publishing platforms. Each has its processes and requirements, so it's wise to research thoroughly or seek advice from publishing professionals. This preparation ensures that the presentation of your story aligns with your intentions and respects your child's memory.

In all its forms, writing offers a powerful means to explore and express the depths of grief while honoring the memory of our lost loved ones. Whether kept private or shared with the world, your written words can serve as a personal sanctuary and a bridge to others, providing comfort and connection in the journey through sorrow. As you continue to write and possibly share your story, let each word, sentence, and page reflect your love for your child and your path toward healing.

8.4 Artistic Expression as a Grief Outlet

Art therapy emerges as a profound gateway for many who tread the path of grief, offering a sanctuary where emotions can be expressed and processed without the need for words. This form of therapy involves using art materials such as paint, clay, or collage to create works that reflect one's emotional state or memories associated with the loss. Making art allows you to externalize feelings that may be too difficult to articulate, providing a visual language for your grief. For many bereaved parents, art therapy facilitates a unique form of healing by enabling them to bring form and color to their experiences, which often helps in understanding and integrating their emotions more fully. Engaging in art therapy under the guidance of a trained therapist can further enhance this healing process. These professionals can help you explore the meanings and emotions behind your artwork, offering insights that might not have been apparent initially. Additionally, art therapy sessions can become a ritualized time for reflection and connection with your child as you create pieces that are both personally significant and expressive of your journey through grief.

Beyond formal therapy, engaging in creative projects at home or within your community can also be therapeutic. Projects like creating a memory book filled with photos and mementos, designing a piece of jewelry that incorporates something significant from your child, or crafting a custom piece of art that depicts a cherished memory, can all be powerful ways to honor your child's memory and express your emotions. These projects keep your hands busy and engage your mind and heart, helping to soothe the ache of absence with the warmth of remembrance. Creating something beautiful from your grief can be a profound testament to the enduring love for your child, transforming pain into something tangible that others can see, touch, and understand.

Whether locally or online, engagement with the arts community can provide additional layers of support and inspiration. Many communities have arts centers, galleries, or online platforms where individuals who have experienced loss gather to share their artworks and stories. Participating in art exhibitions, attending grief-related art workshops, or simply being part of a community that values creative expression can offer comfort and connection. These communities often foster a sense of belonging and understanding, providing a space where the nuances of grief are recognized and respected. For those who may feel isolated in their sorrow, these connections can be particularly healing, as they reaffirm that while your grief is unique, you are not alone in your journey.

The potential for exhibiting art created from your grief journey offers another dimension of healing and connection. Exhibitions dedicated to themes of loss and healing can provide a platform for you to share your journey with a broader audience. This act of sharing can be incredibly validating, as it not only acknowledges your grief but also celebrates the strength and creativity with which you have navigated your loss. Such exhibitions can also facilitate conversations about grief and healing, helping to break down the stigma often associated with talking about loss. For viewers, seeing art that encapsulates such profound emotions can be deeply moving, providing them with new insights into the experience of loss or reflecting on their own experiences.

Artistic expression is a versatile and profound outlet for grief, offering pathways to externalize and process emotions, honor memories, and connect with others. Through art therapy, creative projects, community engagement, and exhibitions, art becomes a bridge that connects the internal world of grief with the external world of expression and understanding. As you explore and engage with art in its many forms, you may find that it helps you cope with your loss and transforms your grief into meaningful and lasting tributes to your child.

In this chapter, we explored how transforming grief into action can significantly impact healing and honoring the memory of a lost child. Bereaved parents can find meaningful ways to channel their grief into positive outcomes through advocacy, establishing foundations, writing, and artistic expression. These actions not only preserve the memory of their children but also provide support, hope, and inspiration to others facing similar losses. As we close this chapter, we look forward to exploring how nurturing relationships after loss can further support healing and growth, continuing to weave the legacy of love and resilience into the fabric of everyday life.

Chapter 9: Nurturing Relationships After Loss

In the labyrinth of grief, where each turn and corner presents its own set of challenges and emotions, the paths we tread with our partners can often become obscured. The profound loss of an adult child : not only your world but also the shared world you've built with your significant other. As both of you navigate this new, unwelcome terrain, finding ways to reconnect with each other, respecting the individual ways you each process grief, and rediscovering shared moments of joy and intimacy can feel like rediscovering the map to a territory that once felt familiar but now seems fraught with new obstacles and hidden snares. While deeply personal, this part of your journey does not have to be walked in solitude but can be a path of mutual rediscovery and healing.

9.1 Reconnecting with Your Partner After Loss

Understanding Different Grieving Styles

In the labyrinth of grief, where each turn and corner presents its own set of challenges and emotions, the paths we tread with our partners can often become obscured. The profound loss of an adult child impacts not only your world but also the shared world you've built with your significant other. As both of you navigate this new, unwelcome terrain, finding ways to reconnect with each other, respecting the individual ways you each process grief, and rediscovering shared moments of joy and intimacy can feel like rediscovering the map to a territory that once felt familiar but now seems fraught with new obstacles and hidden snares. While deeply personal, this part of your journey does not have to be walked in solitude but can be a path of mutual rediscovery and healing.

A Story of Reconnecting Through Shared Grief

When Michael and Jane lost their daughter, Emma, to a sudden illness, their world was shattered. Emma had been the light of their lives, and her absence left a gaping void. Initially, their grief seemed to drive a wedge between them. Michael retreated into silence, unable to talk about his pain, while Jane sought comfort in talking about Emma constantly. Their differing coping mechanisms created a rift, and they drifted apart.

One day, a friend suggested they attend a grief support group together. Reluctantly, they agreed. At first, the sessions were painful, and neither of them felt comfortable sharing. But as they listened to others' stories, they began to see reflections of their own experiences and found comfort in knowing they were not alone.

Gradually, Michael and Jane started to open up in the group and with each other. They discovered

---

The dance of a relationship changes its rhythm when grief enters the scene. You and your partner may find yourselves out of sync, each moving to the beat of your sorrow, which can manifest differently. Recognizing and respecting these differences is crucial. One of you may find solace in silent reflection, while the other finds relief in shared memories and conversations. These disparities can lead to misunderstandings, with each of you perhaps feeling isolated or unsupported by the other. It's essential to acknowledge that there is no right way to grieve, and the differences in your grieving styles aren't indicators of the depth of love or pain felt for the child you both mourn. Openly discussing these differences without judgment can help foster understanding and patience between you and your partner. It allows both of you to grieve in your ways while supporting each other through this journey.

9.2 Communication Strategies

Effective communication becomes even more vital when you and your partner are navigating the complexities of grief. Creating a space where you can express your feelings openly without fear of dismissal or judgment is essential. This might involve setting aside a specific time to discuss your emotions or establishing 'check-in' moments throughout the week. Active listening plays a critical role here—encourage each other to share the emotions and thoughts that are easily expressed and those that are harder to articulate. Remember, this communication is not about finding immediate solutions to grief but about understanding and sharing your emotional journeys, which can significantly strengthen your bond.

Rekindling Intimacy

Loss can strain intimacy, leaving both partners feeling disconnected. It's important to recognize that intimacy isn't solely physical but emotional. Start by rekindling emotional intimacy, which can be as simple as holding hands, sharing your child's memory, or expressing appreciation for each other's support. This emotional closeness can gradually pave the way for physical intimacy, which can also be a powerful expression of love and reaffirm life. Approach this gently and patiently, communicating openly about your needs and readiness. Intimacy can become a healing act, a way of reaffirming the bond that not only survives grief but can grow stronger through it.

Joint Healing Activities

Engaging in activities together can be a therapeutic way to strengthen your relationship while healing. Consider attending support groups where you can meet other couples navigating similar losses. Such groups provide insights and coping strategies, reminding you that you're not alone in your struggles. Simple activities like regular walks in nature can offer fresh air and a new perspective away from the usual environments that may hold strong associations with your child. Participating in memorial activities for your child, such as planting a garden or creating a scrapbook, can also be a powerful way to connect, allowing you both to express your grief while celebrating the life of your child. These shared activities can become pillars of your new routine, providing comfort and continuity in a world that has irrevocably changed.

In nurturing your relationship after losing a child, remember that this process is not about returning to how things were but finding a new way forward together. It's about learning, growing, and healing as a couple, with each step taken side by side and each challenge faced as a team. Through understanding, communication, and shared experiences, the journey of grief can lead to a deeper, more resilient bond, marked not only by the pain of loss but also by the love and support that shines through even in the darkest times.

Supporting Each Other: The Parent-Sibling Relationship

When a family endures the loss of a child, the grief permeates every relationship within that family, affecting each member in unique and profound ways. For parents, the focus often shifts immediately to their heartbreak, but it's essential to recognize and address the grief experienced by surviving siblings. These brothers and sisters lose a sibling and part of their shared future. Acknowledging each sibling's grief is crucial. It's important to remember that children and young adults may express their sorrow differently than adults. Some seem to withdraw into silence, while others might throw themselves into activities or schoolwork as if nothing has changed. As a parent, creating a space that acknowledges these varied expressions of grief is vital. Encourage open dialogue, letting them know that all forms of grief are valid and that it's okay to express their feelings, whatever they may be, without fear of judgment.

Establishing a safe space for open conversations about the loss is another significant step in supporting siblings. This might involve scheduled family meetings where everyone is invited to share their feelings and memories or informal settings like shared meals where conversations about the deceased child can naturally arise. It is helpful to lead by example; by openly sharing your feelings and memories, you can encourage siblings to do the same. This practice helps in processing individual grief and strengthens family bonds, reinforcing the support system that each family member needs during this time. It's also beneficial to integrate creative expressions of grief, such as drawing, writing, or music, which can be particularly effective for younger children who might struggle to articulate their feelings verbally.

Creating shared remembrance practices is a powerful way to foster a sense of unity and collective healing within the family. This could involve annual rituals on the birthday or death anniversary of the deceased, where family members can come together to celebrate their loved son's or daughter's life. Simple activities like lighting candles, releasing balloons with messages, or visiting a place significant to the deceased can be part of these rituals. These acts of shared remembrance serve as a reminder that while the loved one is no longer physically present, their spirit and memories continue to be a part of the family's life.

Lastly, it is critical to recognize when siblings might need external support to cope with their grief. While families can provide immense support, professional help from grief counselors or child psychologists might be necessary to help them process their emotions healthily. Additionally, there are numerous support groups specifically tailored for children and adolescents that can connect them with peers who are experiencing similar losses. These groups can be particularly validating for siblings who feel misunderstood by friends who haven't experienced a similar loss. As a parent, facilitating access to these resources and sometimes even participating in sessions with them can affirm your support for their healing process.

Navigating the complex dynamics of a family in grief requires patience, understanding, and proactive support. By acknowledging each sibling's unique grief, fostering open communication, creating shared remembrance practices, and accessing external support resources, you can help ensure the entire family moves through this challenging time with love and solidarity. These actions are not just about coping with the loss but about rebuilding a family foundation that honors the memory of the deceased child while supporting each member's emotional well-being.

9.3 Friends Who Stay: Nurturing Supportive Friendships

In the aftermath of losing an adult child, the landscape of your friendships can undergo significant shifts. During such times, the true essence of friendship is often illuminated, showing which relationships can withstand the storms of profound grief and which may falter under the weight. Valuing the friends who remain by your side, offering their presence and patience, becomes crucial. These friends may not always know the right things to say or the perfect way to comfort you, but their steadfast presence is a quiet testament to their commitment and care. Their support is most profoundly felt in the simple acts—sitting silently with you, listening as you share memories of your child, or doing everyday tasks alongside you. This companionship can be incredibly comforting, providing a sense of normalcy and unconditional support that is deeply needed during such turbulent times.

However, maintaining these friendships and ensuring they continue to provide support in a way that resonates with your needs requires clear communication. Being open with your friends about the most helpful forms of support is beneficial. Whether you need space to talk about your child, reminisce about past experiences, or simply need the company to feel less alone, letting your friends know can help them support you better. Educating them about your grief process can also help; explaining that grief can be unpredictable and that some days might be harder than others can prepare them to respond with the flexibility and understanding you need. Additionally, setting boundaries is important. If certain topics or situations are too painful, conveying this to your friends can prevent discomfort and misunderstandings, ensuring that the support they intend to give is not inadvertently hurtful.

The dynamic of friendships after such a loss can also evolve, requiring a reinvestment of emotional energy. You may find that some friends become closer through the shared experience of your grief, while others may drift away, unable to meet the emotional demands of the situation. This shift is natural, and although it can be painful, it offers an opportunity to deepen connections with those who truly understand and empathize with your loss. Reinforcing these bonds can involve engaging in activities you both enjoy, inviting them to be part of memorial events for your child, or simply spending time together in ways that foster mutual comfort and joy. These acts of shared experiences can fortify your friendships, turning them into sources of strength and resilience during your healing process.

Furthermore, the journey through grief often opens pathways to new friendships, particularly with individuals who have experienced similar losses. Engaging with support groups or community organizations focused on grief can connect you with others who understand the depth of your sorrow from personal experience. These new connections can be invaluable, providing a space where your feelings of loss are inherently understood and shared. The communal support found in these groups can also offer new perspectives and coping strategies that might differ from those in your existing friendships, enriching your support network. Cultivating these new friendships can be a gentle reminder that you are not alone in your grief and that support can come from unexpected places, offering new companionship and hope as you navigate your path toward healing.

In nurturing these old and new friendships, you weave a support network that can hold you through the darkest times and lead you toward light and recovery. The friends who stay, listen, and support you without judgment are invaluable treasures, reminding you of the enduring power of human connection. As you continue to cultivate these relationships, they not only help you bear the weight of your loss but also accompany you as you slowly rebuild a life touched by both sorrow and profound love.

9.4 New Relationships: Opening Up to New People

In the wake of losing an adult child, the thought of forming new relationships might feel daunting or even unnecessary. However, these new connections can become a vital part of your support system, offering fresh perspectives and empathy to help alleviate the isolation often felt in grief. Engaging with new people requires a level of vulnerability that can be particularly challenging when you are carrying the weight of profound loss. Opening up about your loss and grief journey with new acquaintances isn't just about sharing your story; it's about allowing others to understand the depth of your experience and, in doing so, forging connections rooted in authenticity and mutual respect.

Navigating the vulnerability required in these interactions involves a delicate balance. It's natural to feel protective of your emotions, especially in the early stages of grief when the pain is raw and pervasive. Yet, there is a profound strength in vulnerability. Sharing your story can be cathartic, helping you process and make sense of your loss. However, it is crucial to gauge new acquaintances' comfort level and receptiveness. Start with small disclosures, build up as you feel more comfortable, and sense reciprocal openness. This approach protects your emotional well-being and helps establish boundaries that new relationships need to respect.

The timing of forming new relationships is another aspect that requires careful consideration. There is no set timeline for when you might feel ready to meet new people and let them into your life. It's a deeply personal decision that depends on several factors, including the intensity of your grief and your emotional readiness to engage with others. Listen to your instincts—your emotions will often guide you in understanding whether you're ready to form new connections or need more time to heal in solitude. Engaging in activities and hobbies that interest you can be a natural way to meet new people without the specific intention of forming deep relationships. These interactions, based on shared interests rather than your grief, can gradually lead to meaningful connections.

When you meet people who have experienced similar losses, the potential for deep, empathetic connections is significant. Shared experiences can forge a quick and profound bond, as there is an inherent understanding of the pain and challenges of losing a loved one. However, while shared grief can bring people together, it's important to avoid falling into comparative grief—where conversations may inadvertently turn into comparisons about whose loss is greater or more challenging. Such interactions can be subtly undermining and might detract from the support and understanding each person seeks. Instead, focus on sharing experiences and feelings that help validate and support each other's unique paths through grief.

Introducing the memory of your child into new relationships is a thoughtful process that ensures their legacy continues to be a part of your life. When you share memories of your child, you're not just recounting past events; you're letting new people see your child's profound influence on your life. Choose what you share based on the other person's comfort level and interest. You might start by mentioning your child in relevant conversations or sharing stories that naturally fit into discussions. Over time, as the relationship deepens, more detailed memories and expressions of your ongoing connection to your child can be shared. This gradual approach allows your child's legacy to enter the new relationship respectfully and organically, ensuring it is handled with the care and significance it deserves.

In navigating these new waters, where every interaction holds the potential for connection or retreat, remember that each step towards vulnerability, each decision about timing, and each shared experience is part of reshaping your social world after loss. These new relationships, built on the foundations of mutual understanding and shared experiences, can offer comfort, joy, and a renewed sense of belonging. They remind us that even amid grief, the human capacity for connection remains a powerful force for healing and growth.

As this chapter concludes, we reflect on the essential nature of relationships in the landscape of grief. From intimate connections with partners and family to supportive bonds with friends and tentative steps towards new relationships, each interaction holds the potential to influence our healing journey profoundly. As we move forward, the next chapter will explore the importance of self-care and resilience, essential components in navigating the ongoing challenges of grief and rebuilding a life marked by loss and hope.

Chapter 10: Self-Care and Resilience Building

In the stillness that often accompanies the night, long after the day's distractions have faded, the true toll of grief can become known, manifesting through disrupted sleep, a relentless sense of fatigue, or a body that feels as though it has been drained of its very strength. During these quiet hours, the profound link between our physical being and our emotional state becomes unmistakably clear. This chapter is dedicated to nurturing physical health as a fundamental healing component. In the careful tending to our bodies, it is here that we often find the reserves of strength needed to carry our emotional burdens and, ultimately, foster resilience.

After losing her son, Daniel, to a sudden illness, Maria felt as if the ground had been ripped from beneath her feet. The days blurred into nights, and she struggled to find a reason to get out of bed. The overwhelming grief took a toll on her physically, leading to sleepless nights, loss of appetite, and a constant state of fatigue.

One evening, as Maria lay awake, she remembered how Daniel encouraged her to care for herself. "Mom, you can't pour from an empty cup," he often said. These words echoed in her mind, prompting her to take the first small step towards self-care.

Maria started by incorporating a simple routine into her mourning. She began with gentle stretches, gradually taking short walks around her neighborhood. These walks, initially challenging, became a time for reflection and connection with nature. She found solace in the rhythmic movement, the fresh air, and the simple act of putting one foot in front of the other.

Encouraged by the small improvements in her physical well-being, Maria introduced other self-care practices. She paid attention to her diet, opting for nourishing foods that gave her energy and vitality. She also established a bedtime routine, which included reading a calming book and practicing deep breathing exercises to help her sleep better.

Over time, Maria noticed a significant change. The physical care she was giving herself began to translate into emotional strength. She felt more equipped to face her grief, her resilience gradually building with each self-care practice. Maria's journey towards self-care didn't erase her pain, but it

---

10.1 Physical Health and Grief:

The Mind-Body Connection

Recognizing Physical Symptoms of Grief

In its most intense forms, grief can manifest physically in ways that might surprise you. Common symptoms include fatigue, changes in appetite, unexplained aches, and disturbances in sleep patterns. These physical reactions are your body's response to the stress of loss, a natural response from a system inextricably linked to your emotional health. Recognizing these symptoms not as mere nuisances but as significant indicators of your body's profound connection to your emotional state is vital. Addressing these physical symptoms is not just about alleviating discomfort but about acknowledging and caring for your grief in a holistic manner.

To begin, keep a simple journal where you can note any physical symptoms you experience. This practice will not only help you track patterns and triggers but also serve as a reminder that your physical health needs attention. Sharing this information with healthcare providers can also enhance their support and treatments, ensuring that your care regimen addresses all aspects of your grief, not just the emotional ones.

Nutrition and Exercise

Maintaining nutrition can feel monumental when every meal tastes like ash under the shadow of grief. However, nourishing your body can be an act of self-care that supports both physical and emotional recovery. Start with small, manageable goals, such as including a fruit or vegetable in each meal or drinking a set amount of water daily. This small nourishment can gradually help reinforce your energy levels and overall well-being.

Similarly, exercise might be the last thing on your mind, yet it holds significant benefits for the grieving. Physical activity releases endorphins, the body's natural painkillers, which can lift your mood and improve your health. Begin with gentle activities like walking or yoga, which can also serve as meditative practices to help still your mind and connect with your body in moments of peace.

Rest and Sleep

Sleep is often the first casualty in the battle of grief, with nights either sleepless or filled with restless dreams. Creating a bedtime routine can signal your body that it's time to wind down and rest. This routine might include activities such as reading, light stretching, or listening to calming music. Additionally, consider the environment in which you sleep; a comfortable, soothing atmosphere, free from reminders of your loss, can help improve the quality of your rest. Avoid stimulants such as caffeine close to bedtime and try to keep electronic devices out of the bedroom to minimize distractions.

Regular check-ups with healthcare providers play a crucial role in managing the physical symptoms of grief. These professionals can offer valuable insights into how your body reacts to stress and provide strategies or treatments to help alleviate these symptoms. If you're experiencing severe or persistent symptoms, such as ongoing insomnia or significant weight changes, it's essential to seek professional advice. Sometimes, healthcare providers may also recommend therapies such as massage or acupuncture, which can help release physical tension and promote relaxation.

Proactive self-care requires acknowledging the deep connections between your physical state and your emotional landscape. By nurturing your body, you also care for your grieving heart; each small act of self-care is a step toward healing and resilience. This holistic approach not only supports your journey through grief but also empowers you to reclaim a life marked by well-being and hope, even in the face of profound loss.

10.2 Mental Health Maintenance: Practices for Emotional Stability

In the swirling chaos that often accompanies the loss of an adult child, finding your emotional footing can seem like an insurmountable task. Much like the body, the mind needs tender care and specific strategies to regain stability and health during such turbulent times. Mindfulness and meditation are vital tools in this regard, offering a gentle yet powerful means to anchor your thoughts and calm your spirit. These practices invite you to experience the present moment without the heavy filters of overwhelming grief or anxiety. By focusing on your breath or engaging in guided imagery, you can create a small oasis of calm in your day. This practice doesn't require extensive time commitments; even a few minutes each day can significantly reduce feelings of anxiety and depression, helping you to regain a sense of control and peace amidst the storm of emotions.

Transitioning from mindfulness to more structured therapeutic practices can enhance mental health maintenance. Whether one-on-one or in group settings, counseling provides a safe space to explore your emotions with professional guidance. On the other hand, art therapy allows for expressive healing even when words fail, helping to process grief through creative expression. Journaling serves as a personal therapy session on paper, where you can openly converse with your thoughts and feelings, tracking your emotional evolution and recognizing patterns that might need more focused attention. Regularly engaging in these therapeutic practices helps in processing your grief and builds a framework for enduring emotional health and resilience.

Amidst the unpredictable waves of grief, establishing a routine provides a structure that can be incredibly comforting. A defined routine, whether a morning walk, a set time for meals, or a bedtime ritual, imposes a rhythm to your day that can help counterbalance the erratic nature of mourning. This predictable pattern not only brings a semblance of normalcy; it also reinforces a sense of competence and control over your daily life. Routine can be particularly soothing when life feels overwhelmingly chaotic, providing tangible proof that despite the profound loss, some aspects of life can still be managed and expected to function as planned.

Lastly, an often-overlooked aspect of maintaining mental health during grief is the identification and management of stressors. This might involve taking a close look at your workload, social commitments, and other potential sources of stress. Learning to say no or delegate tasks is not a sign of weakness but a necessary strategy for conserving energy. It's about recognizing that your capacity to handle stress differs and adjusting your responsibilities accordingly. This adjustment helps protect your mental health and provides the space needed for healing and, eventually, for growth. By setting these boundaries, you are honoring your need for healing as much as you manage the practical aspects of your life, ensuring that unnecessary burdens do not hinder your path through grief.

10.3 The Role of Resilience in Grieving Process

Resilience, often visualized as the capacity to bounce back from life's challenges, takes on a profound significance in the context of grieving. It is not merely about returning to a baseline of functioning but involves a dynamic process of ongoing adaptation, learning, and growth in the face of loss. Resilience in grief does not imply a timeline or an end point but a gradual progression through which you continue to integrate the reality of loss into your life while discovering ways to endure and eventually thrive. Building resilience during grief involves nurturing a mindset that accepts the duality of loss—its stark pain and its potential for engendering growth. This mindset can be fostered through practices encouraging emotional expression, connection with others, and personal reflection. Regular engagement in activities that promote psychological flexibility, such as guided meditation focused on acceptance, can also enhance resilience. These practices help maintain an openness to new experiences and emotions, which is crucial for adaptive coping.

Learning from loss is a transformative journey that is pivotal in building resilience. The pain of losing an adult child can reshape your worldview, values, and self-perception. Through this transformative process, many discover a deepened capacity for empathy, having experienced profound sorrow firsthand. This newfound empathy can lead to more meaningful relationships and a deeper appreciation for the fragility and beauty of life. Engaging in volunteer work or support groups where you can share your experiences and support others grieving can be particularly enriching. These activities provide solace and underscore the shared human experience of loss, fostering a sense of community and mutual support. Moreover, embracing creative outlets such as writing, art, or music can give voice to your grief and open up new avenues for personal expression and understanding.

Setting realistic expectations for the grieving process is crucial for developing resilience. Understanding that grief is not a linear process, but a complex, fluctuating experience helps set a realistic framework for your healing journey. It's important to recognize and accept that there will be days of intense sadness or frustration, just as there will be moments of joy or peace. Allowing yourself to experience these emotions without judgment fosters a compassionate self-awareness essential for healing. Educating yourself about the typical stages of grief can also temper expectations, helping you to understand and normalize your experiences. Furthermore, setting small, achievable daily goals can provide a sense of accomplishment and forward movement, vital for maintaining motivation and hope during difficult times.

Finding meaning in loss is perhaps one of the most powerful ways to build resilience. This may involve framing your loss experience within a larger narrative of love and legacy, focusing on the memories and bonds that continue to impact your life positively. Many find comfort and purpose in activities that honor their child's memory, such as fundraising for a cause they were passionate about or starting a community project in their name. These actions create a legacy that transcends the pain of loss, offering a tangible expression of love that endures. Reflecting on personal values and beliefs and how they have been shaped by the experience of loss can also contribute to a meaningful narrative that guides your actions and choices moving forward. This ongoing search for meaning enriches your purpose and reinforces your capacity to navigate life's challenges with resilience and grace.

By actively engaging in these practices, you gradually weave the threads of resilience through the fabric of your grief, transforming how you interact with the world and yourself in the aftermath of loss. This process is not about diminishing the pain or the significance of your loss but about enriching your life's tapestry with the strength, wisdom, and compassion that comes from having loved and grieved deeply.

10.4 Creating a Personalized Self-Care Routine

In the landscape of grief, where each day may seem challenging, establishing a personalized self-care routine provides a framework for daily living and a pathway to healing that respects your unique needs and circumstances. Self-care extends beyond the basics of health; it encompasses a broad spectrum of activities and practices that nourish your entire being—body, mind, and spirit. Understanding and honoring your specific needs in these areas can transform routine acts into profound rituals of self-compassion and recovery.

Assessing Personal Needs

The first step in crafting a personalized self-care routine is a thoughtful assessment of your current needs, likely to differ from those you had before your loss. This assessment should consider several physical, emotional, and spiritual dimensions contributing to overall well-being. Physically, you might need more rest or specific types of nutrition. Emotionally, the need could be for therapeutic activities that help process feelings or for practices that reduce stress. Spiritually, you might seek deeper connections or need quiet time for reflection. Evaluating these needs isn't a one-time task but an ongoing process, as they will likely shift as you move through different stages of grief. Keeping a journal where you can note your feelings, physical state, and spiritual insights daily can help you track these shifts and adjust your care routine accordingly.

Incorporating Joyful Activities

Integrating activities that bring you joy and relaxation is essential to effective self-care. Joyful activities light up your spirit and bring a sense of satisfaction and happiness. This could be anything from gardening, reading, painting, listening to music, dancing, or watching favorite movies. The key is to allow yourself moments where grief can be put aside, allowing you to bask in activities that bring happiness. These moments are not about forgetting your loss but about permitting yourself to enjoy life amidst the grief, acknowledging that joy and sorrow can coexist. Making these activities a regular part of your routine can help balance the heaviness of mourning with the lightness of pleasure, contributing to emotional resilience.

Social Connections

The role of social connections in self-care is crucial; humans are inherently social beings, and isolation can exacerbate the feelings of loneliness that often accompany grief. While the inclination might be to withdraw into your shell, maintaining social contacts can provide significant emotional support. This doesn't mean you must keep a busy social calendar—it's about quality, not quantity. Focus on supportive and empathetic relationships, perhaps a friend who listens well, a family member who understands your need for quiet companionship, or a fellow bereaved parent who shares your loss experience. Additionally, consider joining a support group to connect with others who are navigating similar paths. These connections can offer validation, reduce feelings of isolation, and provide opportunities to share coping strategies.

Adapting Self-Care Over Time

As you journey through grief, your self-care needs will evolve, and so will your self-care routine. What helps in the immediate aftermath of loss might not feel as effective several months later. This evolution is a normal part of the healing process. Regularly re-evaluating your routine is essential to ensure that it continues to meet your changing needs. Be open to trying new self-care strategies and modifying existing ones. Flexibility in your self-care routine accommodates your changing needs and introduces a dynamic element to your healing process, aligning it with your personal growth and current emotional landscape.

Crafting a personalized self-care routine is not about adhering strictly to self-imposed rules but about creating a flexible framework that supports your healing. It's about making conscious daily choices that honor and nurture all aspects of your being, helping you recover from your loss with time, intentionality, and self-compassion.

In wrapping up this chapter, we've explored the intricate art of crafting a self-care routine that honors the multifaceted nature of your grief. From assessing your varied needs to integrating joy and maintaining social connections, each element of your routine serves as a stepping stone toward recovery. As we transition from focusing on self-care to exploring the enduring bonds and legacies left by those we've lost, remember that self-care is not a selfish act but a necessary one, ensuring that you have the strength and resilience to continue loving, remembering, and living.

Chapter 11: Honoring and Remembering While Moving Forward

A Story of Creating a Memory Project

When Karen lost her daughter, Lily, to a tragic accident, she was overwhelmed by a sense of emptiness and a desperate need to keep Lily's memory alive. Karen wanted to find a way to honor Lily's life in a tangible manner that would not only keep her daughter's spirit close but also help her navigate her grief.

Karen decided to create a memory quilt, a project that would weave together pieces of Lily's life into a comforting, tangible tribute. She gathered Lily's favorite T-shirts, concert tickets, and scraps of fabric from significant moments in her daughter's life. Each piece she selected held a story, a memory, a fragment of Lily's vibrant presence.

As Karen began stitching the quilt, she found the process therapeutic. The act of sewing each piece together allowed her to reflect on the beautiful moments she shared with Lily. It became a meditative practice, offering solace and a sense of connection. Each square of the quilt told a story, and together, they created a tapestry of Lily's life that Karen could wrap around herself, literally and metaphorically, during moments of profound sorrow.

Karen's memory quilt became more than just a blanket; it was a living testament to Lily's life, a source of comfort, and a way to keep her daughter's memory alive. It helped Karen navigate her grief by giving her a purpose and a way to transform her sorrow into something beautiful and meaningful.

As dawn gently breaks over the horizon, it reminds us of the inevitable passage of time, a fresh day that greets us all, irrespective of our burdens or joys. For you, as a parent who has endured the profound loss of an adult child, each new day can feel like a delicate negotiation between honoring the precious memories of your child and finding the strength to move forward. In this chapter, we explore tangible and heartfelt ways to maintain a connection to your child, transforming your enduring love and memories into lasting tributes that honor their life and pave a path toward healing.

11.1 Memory Projects: Tangible Acts of Remembrance

With its gentle yet persistent presence, memory can serve as a powerful medium for healing. Engaging in creative memory projects allows you to channel your grief into making something beautiful and enduring that reflects the essence of your child. Scrapbooking, for example, is a profoundly personal way to compile memories, photographs, and mementos that tell the story of your child's life. Each page can be a canvas for expressions of love, significant milestones, or everyday moments you cherished together. Similarly, quilting can transform your child's clothes—perhaps a favorite t-shirt, a team jersey, or a well-worn scarf—into a comforting, tangible quilt that envelops you with memories.

The digital realm offers an expansive canvas for remembrance as well. Creating a digital memory archive can include everything from a collection of digital photos and videos to an interactive blog or website dedicated to your child. This digital space can serve as a personal repository of memories and a way to share your child's story with a broader audience, connecting with others who may draw comfort and inspiration from your reflections.

Public Memorials: Anchors in the Community

Public memorials, such as park benches or commemorative plaques, provide a physical space in the community where your child's memory can be honored and visited by those whose lives they touched. Creating a public memorial typically involves selecting a meaningful location—perhaps a favorite park, a school campus, or a community center. Collaborating with local authorities, you can determine the feasibility of your project and understand the necessary steps, which might include fundraising, designing, and planning a dedication ceremony. These memorials offer a lasting legacy that commemorates your child's life and provides a place of solace and reflection for the community.

Anniversary Rituals: Marking Time with Meaning

Anniversaries, birthdays, and significant dates naturally stir memories and emotions. Creating rituals or activities to mark these dates can turn them into memorable moments of remembrance and celebration. You might light a candle every year at the exact hour of your child's birth or perhaps release biodegradable lanterns into the sky. Some families find comfort in gathering together to share stories, watch a favorite movie of their loved one, or prepare a meal their child loved. These rituals, repeated annually, help weave your child's memory into the fabric of everyday life, acknowledging their lasting impact on your family.

Legacy Projects: Building Futures in Their Name

Consider establishing a scholarship in your child's name at their alma mater or creating a foundation that supports a cause they were passionate about. These legacy projects do more than memorialize your child; they create opportunities for others, extending the positive influences of your child's life into the future. Engaging in these projects can provide a focus for your grief, turning it into motivational energy that helps others and keeps your child's spirit active in the world.

Undertaking these memory projects and establishing lasting memorials are acts of love that honor your child's life and legacy. They serve as reminders that although your child is no longer physically present, their influence, dreams, and memories continue to live on, both in your heart and in the world around you. Through these acts of remembrance, you forge a new relationship with your child—one that is not defined by their absence but enriched by the enduring presence of their memory in your life and the lives of others.

11.2 Incorporating Memories into Daily Life

In the gentle ebb and flow of daily life, where moments pass by sometimes unnoticed, the memory of a loved one can serve as a poignant reminder of both the love shared and the permanence of loss. Integrating small, tangible reminders of your child into your daily routine can be a subtle yet powerful way to honor their memory while weaving their essence into the fabric of your everyday life. Consider wearing a piece of jewelry—a locket containing a photo of your child or a bracelet intertwined with a symbol representing something significant about them. Each time you touch or see the piece, it's not just a reminder of their absence but a small, personal acknowledgment of their ongoing presence in your life. Similarly, carrying a keepsake, such as a keychain crafted from something they owned or a small book they loved, can provide a sense of closeness and continuity.

The spaces we inhabit also resonate with memories and creating dedicated areas within your home that reflect and honor your child can transform ordinary spaces into sanctuaries of remembrance. This could be as simple as dedicating a corner of a room for their photographs, cherished possessions, or awards. Alternatively, it might involve more elaborate setups like a shelf displaying their personal items, books, or a collection of vinyl records they adored. These memory spaces can become focal points for reflection, offering a physical space to connect with memories of your child. Lighting a candle there during significant dates or whenever you need closeness can be a comforting ritual, illuminating the space with warmth and love.

Sharing stories about your child is crucial in keeping their memory vibrant. Encourage conversations about your child with family and friends, recounting anecdotes or traits that encapsulate who they were. These stories can be shared during family gatherings, through social media, or even integrated into family events, ensuring that your child's life stories continue to echo within the lives of those they touched. This act of sharing not only keeps your child's memory alive but also allows others to understand the depth of your loss and the profoundness of the bond you shared. It can be therapeutic for you and those who hear the stories, fostering a shared connection and communal healing.

Balancing the natural desire to remember your child with the necessity to continue living your life presents a delicate challenge. It involves acknowledging the pain of loss and allowing yourself to experience joy and embrace life's ongoing journey. This balance does not diminish your love for your child; instead, it honors their desire for your happiness as much as you honor their memory. Embracing moments of joy does not signify moving on from your child's memory but rather moving forward with it, allowing their memory to accompany you in new experiences and joys. This approach to living after loss is not about forgetting but about transforming grief into a loving tribute that acknowledges the past while engaging with the present.

Incorporating these practices into your daily life keeps your child's memory alive and integrates your experience of loss into a narrative of continued love and connection. It is a testament to the enduring impact of your child's life, a life that continues to influence, inspire, and move you, reshaping your world in miniature, meaningful ways each day.

11.3 The Concept of Continuing Bonds

The loss of an adult child is an experience that reshapes your existence in profound ways, leaving you to navigate a world that feels irrevocably altered. In seeking a path that honors both your love and your loss, you may discover the concept of continuing bonds, a therapeutic notion that encourages maintaining an ongoing relationship with your loved one despite their physical absence. This concept challenges the traditional notion of "letting go" of the deceased and instead embraces the idea that love does not end with death. Maintaining a connection with your child can be a vital part of your adaptation process, helping you to integrate the loss into your life in a way that feels respectful and true to your relationship.

Creative expression offers a powerful avenue for fostering these continuing bonds. Writing letters to your child can be a profoundly cathartic practice, allowing you to express thoughts and emotions that you wish to share with them. These letters can cover daily happenings, share personal achievements or challenges, or convey that they are missed and remembered. This act of writing not only serves as a bridge across the divide of death but also as a tangible manifestation of your ongoing conversation with your child. Similarly, creating art in honor of your child can transform your grief into a visual or auditory expression that communicates your inner experiences and keeps your memory alive in daily life. Whether through painting, music, or sculpture, each creation is a testament to your child's lasting impact on your world.

Spiritual or religious beliefs often play a crucial role in supporting the concept of continuing bonds. Many find comfort in believing their child's spirit remains present and accessible despite physical absence. Prayer, meditation, or rituals can provide a structured way to engage with these beliefs, offering moments of connection that feel sacred and personal. These practices might include visiting a special place you associate with your child, celebrating their life during religious ceremonies, or simply speaking to them during private moments of reflection. The spiritual connection reaffirmed through these activities can provide profound comfort and solace, reinforcing the presence of your child in your spiritual life.

Communicating the significance of these continuing bonds to others can sometimes be challenging, especially if those around you adhere to different beliefs about grief and memory. It might be helpful to share your feelings and practices openly with friends and family, explaining how these actions help you cope and honor your child's memory. Educating those close to you about continuing bonds can also help them understand your needs and support you in maintaining these connections. Additionally, engaging in discussions with bereavement groups Or online communities can provide further validation and share strategies for nurturing these bonds. Sharing your approach helps others understand your process and invites them to explore their ways of connecting with lost loved ones, fostering a broader understanding of grief and remembrance.

In embracing the concept of continuing bonds, you allow the relationship with your child to evolve into a new form that respects the reality of their absence while affirming the enduring nature of love. This approach does not negate the pain of loss but offers a way to weave this loss into the fabric of your life, acknowledging that the bonds of love are not severed by death but transformed. Through creative expression, spiritual practices, and open communication, you continue to celebrate and honor your child, ensuring that their presence is maintained in memory and the ongoing narrative of your life.

11.4 Celebrating Life Milestones Without Your Child

With its relentless forward motion, life brings milestones that mark the passage of time—graduations, weddings, and the arrival of grandchildren. These significant events, while joyous, can also cast a long shadow of sorrow for you as a parent who has experienced the profound loss of an adult child. Your child's absence during these moments can feel particularly acute, a poignant reminder of what could have been. Navigating these milestones necessitates a delicate balance between honoring the joy of the occasion and acknowledging the grief that such celebrations may reawaken.

Facing these milestones without your child requires a compassionate acknowledgment of your emotions. It's natural to feel a complex mix of joy for the occasion and sadness for your child's absence. Allow yourself to experience these feelings without judgment. Embracing your emotions as they come can be vital in managing them more effectively. Preparing mentally and emotionally for these events can help; consider speaking with a counselor or a supportive friend ahead of time to articulate and process your feelings. This preparation can make the actual day more manageable, allowing you to be present and participate in the joy of the occasion while still honoring your inner experience of loss.

Incorporating your child's memory into these milestones can also provide a meaningful way to acknowledge their absence while celebrating their life. Simple tributes, such as reserving a seat with a meaningful item or photo of your child, can serve as a powerful reminder of their presence in spirit. During weddings, consider including a moment of remembrance in the ceremony or a mention in the wedding program. For graduations or other achievements, dedicating a moment of silence or sharing a favorite memory can allow space for their memory to shine, reminding everyone of their lasting impact on the family and community.

Self-Care During Milestones:

Nurturing Your Emotional Well-Being

The emotional charge of these milestones necessitates prioritizing your self-care. This focus on self-care is not just about coping with the day but about nurturing your well-being throughout the period surrounding the event. Start by recognizing your limits and setting clear boundaries about your participation; stepping away or limiting your involvement is okay if you feel overwhelmed. Engage in practices that ground and center you—deep breathing, mindfulness, or even a brief walk outside during the event can help manage feelings of anxiety or sadness. Additionally, enlisting the support of understanding friends or family members who acknowledge your loss and offer compassion can provide an essential safety net, allowing you to engage with the event at your own pace.

Sharing with New Acquaintances: Bridging Understanding

As life introduces you to new people—perhaps friends of your surviving children or new in-laws at a wedding—the question of how to share your child's memory with those who never knew them arises. This sharing is delicate; it requires gauging the appropriate moments and the receptiveness of others. A practical approach is to share meaningful anecdotes that resonate with the occasion or reflect values or characteristics that your child embodied. Such sharing honors your child's memory and invites new acquaintances to appreciate the depth of your family's tapestry, woven with threads of joy, loss, and enduring love.

Navigating life's milestones without your child is an exercise in balancing grief with celebration and memory with presence. By allowing space for your emotions, incorporating your child's memory into celebrations, practicing diligent self-care, and sharing your child's story, you can honor their life and your journey in a way that feels authentic and healing. This approach does not diminish the pain of their absence but offers a way to celebrate their lasting impact and the continuous love that weaves through every aspect of your life.

As this chapter closes, we reflect on the importance of maintaining the delicate balance between honoring your lost child's memory and embracing life's ongoing joys. The strategies discussed here serve as a guide for navigating challenging moments and a testament to the enduring strength and love that characterize the bereavement journey. Looking ahead, the next chapter will explore the broader implications of building a legacy of love and healing, ensuring that the memories and lessons from your child's life continue to inspire and influence long into the future.

Chapter 12: Building a Legacy of Love and Healing

When Sarah lost her son, Ethan, in a tragic accident, her world was shattered. Ethan had always been a vibrant, compassionate young man with a deep love for the environment. As Sarah navigated her grief, she felt an overwhelming need to keep Ethan's memory alive in a way that honored his passions and the values he held dear.

In the quiet, reflective moments of her grief, Sarah created a legacy project reflecting Ethan's love for nature and his commitment to environmental conservation. She envisioned a community garden that would beautify the neighborhood and serve as a living tribute to Ethan's life and values.

Sarah began by reaching out to friends, family, and community members, sharing her vision and inviting them to participate. The response was overwhelmingly positive, with many people eager to contribute their time, resources, and support. Together, they selected a plot of land in a local park that had been neglected and overgrown with weeds.

The project quickly gained momentum. Volunteers of all ages came together to clear the land, prepare the soil, and plant various native plants and flowers. They installed benches and walking paths, creating a peaceful space where visitors could reflect and connect with nature. To honor Ethan's memory, they planted a tree in the garden's center and placed a plaque beneath it inscribed with his name and a quote that had always inspired him: "The Earth does not belong to us; we belong to the Earth."

As the garden took shape, Sarah found solace in the physical work and the sense of community that surrounded her. The act of creating something beautiful and meaningful from her grief helped her to process her loss and find a renewed sense of purpose. She saw the garden as a living testament to Ethan's life, a place where his spirit would continue to inspire and bring joy to others.

The community garden soon became a cherished part of the neighborhood. It provided a space for children to play, for families to gather, and for individuals to find peace and reflection. Local schools incorporated the garden into their environmental education programs, teaching students about the importance of conservation and the beauty of nature. Sarah took comfort in knowing that Ethan's legacy was positively impacting the community, fostering a deeper connection to the environment and to each other.

In addition to the garden, Sarah organized an annual event called "Ethan's Earth Day," where volunteers came together to clean up local parks, plant trees, and educate the community about sustainable living practices. The event grew each year, drawing participants from all over the city and raising funds for environmental projects. Ethan's passion for the environment ignited a movement that continued to grow, driven by the love and memories of those who knew him.

Through the creation of the community garden and the annual Earth Day event, Sarah found a way to honor Ethan's memory while also making a meaningful contribution to the world. Her journey from grief to action was not easy, but it was filled with moments of healing, connection, and hope. By channeling her sorrow into a legacy of love and healing, Sarah ensured that Ethan's spirit would live on, touching the lives of countless others and

---

As dawn gently breaks over the horizon, it reminds us of the inevitable passage of time, a fresh day that greets us all, irrespective of our burdens or joys. For you, as a parent who has endured the profound loss of an adult child, each new day can feel like a delicate negotiation between honoring the precious memories of your child and finding the strength to move forward. In this chapter, we explore tangible and heartfelt ways to maintain a connection to your child, transforming your enduring love and memories into lasting tributes that honor their life and pave a path toward healing.

12.1 Legacy Through Story: Sharing Your Child's Story

The Power of Storytelling

In the quiet spaces of our hearts, where the echoes of a loved one's laughter once filled the air, storytelling is a profound way to bridge the past with the present and future. Sharing the narrative of your child's life—the joys, challenges, and undeniable impact they had on those around them—serves not just as a cathartic exercise for you, the storyteller, but also as a beacon of strength and hope for others who might be navigating their landscapes of grief. Recounting your child's story in vivid detail can breathe life into their memory, allowing their spirit to continue influencing the world in meaningful ways.

Whether through a heartfelt blog post, a passionately delivered speech at a community event, or chapters in a book, each platform offers a unique avenue for your child's legacy to flourish. Engaging with these platforms allows you to articulate the depth of your love and the pain of your loss while also celebrating the essence of your child's life. This practice keeps their memory vibrant and connects them with others who, on hearing your story, may find the courage to share their own, thus creating a powerful ripple effect of healing and mutual support.

Creating a Platform

Navigating the digital age offers unprecedented opportunities to create platforms where stories can be told and legacies celebrated. Starting a blog or a website dedicated to your child can serve as a focal point for your storytelling efforts, providing a space where family, friends, and even strangers can learn about your child's life and the impact they left behind. Here, you can share everything from detailed accounts of their accomplishments and character to daily reflections and milestones. For those who feel a book might capture the essence of their child's story more fully, self-publishing offers a pathway to bring personal narratives to a broader audience, allowing your child's life story to inspire and resonate with others globally.

Privacy Considerations

While sharing your child's story openly can be healing, it's crucial to navigate the balance between public sharing and private grieving. Establishing boundaries around what you choose to share is essential. Consider aspects of your child's life and your family's experiences that might be too sensitive or personal to place in the public domain. Keeping specific memories for yourself or close family and friends is okay. When setting up a blog, website, or social media page, utilize privacy settings to control who can view or interact with your content, ensuring that you feel comfortable and secure with how your child's story is shared.

Inspiring Others

The stories we share have the potential to touch lives, inspire change, and offer comfort to those walking similar paths of grief. By sharing your child's story, you preserve their memory and offer insights and support to others experiencing the pain of loss. Your child's story could encourage someone to seek help, connect with others, or feel less alone in their sorrow. Moreover, your bravery in sharing openly can empower others to do the same, fostering a community of support and understanding that transcends individual experiences of grief.

In sharing your child's story, you weave a tapestry of memory that honors their existence and asserts that love endures, transforming loss into a legacy of love and healing. Through this legacy, your child continues to make an indelible mark on the world, and their life's story is a testament to the resilience of the human spirit and the transformative power of love.

12.2 Community Projects:

Fostering a Legacy of Giving

In the wake of loss, transforming grief into a constructive force can profoundly impact both the bereaved and the community.

Establishing community projects that reflect the values and interests of your child not only serves as a living tribute but also fosters a sense of purpose and continuity in your life. Identifying meaningful projects might begin with reflecting on what mattered most to your child—environmental conservation, education, art, or animal welfare. Envision a project that aligns with these passions; for example, if your child is an avid reader, consider setting up a book donation drive or funding library resources in underserved communities. Alternatively, if they cared deeply about the environment, initiating a local green space cleanup or tree-planting event can extend their legacy in tangible, life-affirming ways.

Bringing these projects to life often involves collaborating with established organizations or charities with similar goals. Start by researching local or national groups engaged in the relevant areas of interest. Reach out to discuss how a partnership can amplify the impact of your proposed project, ensuring that your efforts are sustainable and well-supported. When selecting an organization to collaborate with, consider their mission alignment, resource availability, and community impact. Adequate collaboration pools resources and combines expertise, expanding the reach and depth of the project. For instance, partnering with a local school for a scholarship fund in your child's name harnesses the school's educational insight while honoring your child's passion for education.

Engaging the community and fundraising are critical components of sustaining any legacy project. Transparent communication about the project's goals, significance, and the lasting impact envisioned can rally community support and participation. Utilize social media platforms, community bulletin boards, and local media to spread the word and invite participation. Hosting community events, such as charity runs, art exhibitions, or bake sales, can generate funds while raising awareness about the cause. Additionally, setting up digital fundraising campaigns through platforms like GoFundMe can reach donors beyond the local community, broadening the support network and increasing the project's visibility and impact.

Measuring the impact of these projects is crucial for maintaining momentum and demonstrating the value of the community's investment. Develop clear, measurable goals at the outset, such as the number of trees planted, scholarships awarded, or pounds of waste collected. Regular updates showcasing progress towards these goals can keep the community engaged and invested in the project's success. Celebrate milestones publicly and acknowledge the contributions of all participants, reinforcing a collective commitment to the legacy being built. This honors your child's memory and demonstrates the tangible outcomes of channeling grief into positive community action. By measuring and celebrating each achievement, you reaffirm the enduring influence of your child's life, inspiring continued support and participation in a legacy that truly embodies the spirit of giving and love.

12.3 Healing Circles: Creating Spaces for Shared Grief

In the tender aftermath of losing a child, the need for shared understanding and emotional support becomes more pronounced. Healing circles, rooted in the ancient tradition of communal gatherings, offer a unique space where emotions can be expressed and shared without judgment. These circles provide a haven where stories of loss and love are intertwined, creating a tapestry of Shared experiences that can significantly alleviate the isolation that often accompanies grief. The benefits of participating in a healing circle are manifold; they provide a structured yet flexible setting where you can openly share your grief, learn from the experiences of others, and receive the kind of support that only those who have faced similar losses can offer.

Organizing and guiding a healing circle requires thoughtfulness and intention to ensure that the space remains respectful and compassionate. Begin by setting clear intentions for each session, which might include providing support, sharing experiences, or collectively finding ways to cope with grief. It is crucial to establish ground rules that prioritize confidentiality and respect for each participant's unique grief process. Creating a safe space goes beyond the emotional and psychological—it also involves choosing a physical environment that is comfortable and inviting, perhaps a quiet room with soft lighting and ample seating that encourages a sense of closeness and security. As the facilitator, your role is pivotal. You guide the discussion with sensitivity, ensuring that each member has a chance to speak and be heard. This might involve sometimes gently steering conversations to ensure they are inclusive and supportive or providing prompts that encourage reflection and sharing. Your presence ensures a safe and supportive environment for everyone.

The advent of digital communication offers new opportunities for those who might not have access to local support groups or who find in-person gatherings challenging. Virtual healing circles can be formed using video conferencing tools, which allow participants to connect from the comfort of their homes while still benefiting from seeing and hearing each other, which can be more personal and connecting than text-based communication. When setting up an online circle, pay attention to the technical aspects that can impact the flow of the session, such as ensuring all participants are familiar with the technology and establishing guidelines for speaking to avoid interruptions. The flexibility of online meetings also allows people from different geographical locations to gather, share their experiences, and support each other, expanding the reach of your healing circle far beyond local boundaries. With virtual healing circles, you have the power to connect and heal, regardless of where you are.

Sustaining a healing circle over time requires commitment and creativity. Regular meetings help build community and trust, which is vital for deep and meaningful exchanges. To maintain engagement, vary the themes of discussions and incorporate rituals that resonate with the group, such as lighting candles for remembrance or holding moments of silence. Encouraging members to take on roles within the group, such as leading a session or sharing a meaningful activity, can foster a sense of ownership and commitment to the circle. Celebrating milestones together, like the anniversaries of loved ones' passings or significant group achievements, can also strengthen bonds and affirm the value of the circle in each member's journey through grief.

In these healing circles, whether seated together in a quiet room or connected by the pixels on a screen, you find a powerful affirmation of the shared human experience. Here, in the collective embrace of those who understand, you find not only support and understanding but also a place where the love for your child can be expressed and remembered, a sacred space where healing can gently unfold, one story, one tear, and one smile at a time.

12.4 A Future Enriched by Memory: Embracing Hope and Joy

In the realms of profound loss, where the shadows of grief often loom large, finding points of light becomes essential—not just for survival but for thriving. With each memory of your child, a spark of joy can be reignited, illuminating paths to a future where hope resides alongside sorrow. Embracing this duality where joy complements grief, rather than diminishing it, allows you to form a new understanding of happiness—one that honors the impact of your child's life.

Finding Hope

Hope, in the aftermath of losing your beloved child, might initially seem like a foreign concept. However, it often resides in the everyday reminders of their life and legacy. You can start to rediscover hope by creating moments in your day that are dedicated to reflection and connection with your child. This might be as simple as watching the sunrise while reminiscing about moments shared or listening to a favorite song they loved, allowing the memories to bring a smile amid the tears. Another powerful way to cultivate hope is by setting goals that align with your child's values or passions. This could be anything from volunteering at organizations they supported to continuing a project they were passionate about. Each step forward in these endeavors keeps their memory alive and rebuilds your sense of purpose and progress, lighting your way through the grief with hope and intention.

Enriching Life with Memories

Memories are the threads that connect us to those we've lost, woven into the fabric of our lives. Keeping the memory of your child vibrant can be an enriching experience that strengthens your connection to them. Consider creating a memory book with photos, stories, and mementos that celebrate their life. Regularly adding to this book can become a therapeutic activity, a way to document the ongoing journey you shared. Additionally, incorporating your child's favorite activities into your routine—cooking their preferred dishes on special occasions or watching films they adored—can transform everyday moments into meaningful connections. These acts of remembrance are gentle affirmations that your child's influence continues to enrich your life, providing comfort and joy amidst the sorrow.

New Traditions

As time progresses, establishing new traditions can offer a way to honor your child's memory while making room for new memories. These traditions might include an annual gathering to celebrate their life with friends and family or a quiet afternoon of reflection in a place that was special to them. Each new tradition bridges the past and the future, acknowledging the loss while embracing the continuation of life. These rituals can evolve, adapting to your healing process and reflecting your relationship with your child, even in their absence. Embracing these new practices keeps your child's memory alive and integrates their spirit into your life's new chapters.

Legacy of Love

The legacy of love you build in your child's memory becomes a testament to their enduring impact. This legacy, crafted from the love, lessons, and memories they left behind, supports not only your journey of healing but also affects those around you. By engaging with life positively, motivated by the love for your child, you inspire others to find strength in their struggles. This legacy does not negate the reality of the pain or the depth of the loss but offers a way to channel grief into actions that affirm life and honor the deep bonds of love that loss cannot sever.

In cultivating these gardens of memory and hope, you do more than cope with grief—you transform it into a force of love and resilience that nourishes your life and the lives of others around you. As this chapter closes, we see not an end but a horizon—a promise that the love shared with your child continues to shape a future prosperous with meaning and joy, a vibrant legacy that is a testament to the transformative power of love and memory.

Conclusion

A woman named Eliza lived in the small coastal town of Haven's Bay, where the whispers of the sea seemed to carry both solace and sorrow. She had weathered the storms of life with grace, but none had tested her as deeply as the loss of her beloved daughter, Lily.

Eliza's journey through grief was a tumultuous one, marked by days where the weight of sorrow threatened to drown her and others where memories of Lily's laughter danced like sunlight on the waves. She sought solace in the words of books, finding comfort in the shared experiences of others who had walked similar paths.

As the seasons passed, Eliza was drawn to a small bookstore between the bustling harbor and the quiet, windswept cliffs. There, among shelves laden with stories of love and loss, she found a book that would change her life.

The book, titled "Survive the Death of an Adult Child," seemed to call out to Eliza, its pages filled with wisdom and understanding. Each chapter spoke to her in ways she couldn't fully explain, as if the author had reached through time and space to offer guidance.

With each turn of the page, Eliza nodded in recognition, her heart swelling with a mixture of sadness and hope. She read about the nonlinear nature of grief, the importance of self-care and mindfulness, and the power of creating a legacy of love.

Inspired by the words in the book, Eliza began weaving Lily's memory into the fabric of her daily life. She planted a garden filled with her daughter's favorite flowers, tended to it carefully, and watched as it blossomed into a vibrant tapestry of color and life.

But Eliza's journey didn't end there. Drawing strength from the stories within the book, she embarked on a mission to honor Lily's memory in a way that would make a difference in the lives of others. With the help of her community, she launched a scholarship fund for local students pursuing their dreams, a legacy of love and purpose that would endure long after she was gone.

As we near the end of our journey together through this book, we must pause and reflect on the path we've traversed—from the initial, overwhelming wave of grief to the more serene shores of healing and acceptance. Grief, as we've explored, is profoundly non-linear. It ebbs and flows, bringing with it days of sharp pain and unexpected moments of respite. This journey is deeply personal yet universally understood by those who walk this path.

Throughout these pages, we've shared theories and concepts and the deeply personal stories of those who have navigated their landscapes of loss. These narratives serve as a testament to the resilience of the human spirit and the transformative power of sharing our experiences.

Each story has a piece of wisdom, a fragment of pain, and a spark of hope that can light the way for others.

We've discussed coping strategies, such as simple self-care and mindfulness, to create lasting memorials and legacy projects. Each strategy is a tool, a potential way to bear the weight of grief a little more easily. Remember, creating, remembering, and celebrating are not just about preservation but active healing.

For many, the journey of grief is also spiritual. Exploring your beliefs can provide a comforting framework to view the loss. Whether through organized religion, personal spirituality, or quiet contemplation, finding meaning beyond the pain can be a powerful aid in your healing process.

One of the most poignant ways to honor your lost child's memory is through actions that forge a legacy of love and purpose. Whether by launching a community project, establishing a scholarship, or simply living in a way that reflects their values, these actions keep their spirit alive. I encourage you to take steps toward building this legacy in whatever way feels right. Not only does it serve as a bridge between past and present, but it also offers hope and connection to the future.

Hope—this is the essence of what I wish for you. The hope that moments of joy and purpose still flicker and flourish amidst the shadows of grief. The hope is that you will find ways to weave your child's memory into the fabric of your daily life, allowing their legacy to inspire and uplift others.

As you continue, remember that grief may never entirely 'end,' but it does change. It becomes a part of who you are, influencing how you see and interact with the world. Give yourself the grace to feel, grieve, and gradually heal.

I invite you to share your own stories of loss and resilience. You find your own healing and light the way for others, offering them comfort and understanding. Together, our stories weave a tapestry of shared human experience, rich with pain, beauty, and the enduring strength of love.

Thank you for allowing me to accompany you through these pages. I sincerely hope you have found understanding, solace, and perhaps a way forward. For further support, remember that counseling services, support groups, and online communities can offer continuous comfort and guidance. You are not alone in this journey.

In solidarity and with heartfelt empathy,

G.M. Grace

May we all find peace, embrace life's complexities, and honor those we have loved and lost with every step we take.

Make a Difference with Your Review

Unlock the Power of Generosity

"Money can't buy happiness, but giving it away can." - Anonymous

---

Helping others selflessly leads to greater fulfillment, a longer life, and more success. We want to provide you with that experience as you read this book. That's why we have a simple question for you:

Would you help someone you've never met, even if it didn't cost you money and you never received any credit for it?

If your answer is yes, we have a request on behalf of someone you don't know – and probably never will.

They are just like you, or like the person you were a few years ago: eager to heal, passionate about finding hope, and searching for guidance. This is where you can help.

To achieve our mission of empowering people in mourning, we need to reach them. Since most people judge books by their cover (and reviews), we kindly ask you to take a brief moment and leave an honest review. It will cost you nothing and take less than 60 seconds.

Your review will help:

- One more grieving parent finds the support they need.

- One more person experiences a transformation they never thought possible.

- Countless lives change for the better.

You only need to spend less than 60 seconds leaving a review to make this happen.

Click this link or go to http://amazon.com/

P.S. If you believe this book can help others, please share it with fellow grieving parents to spread goodwill.

Thank you from the bottom of our hearts!

G.M. Grace

References

10 Grief Counseling Therapy Techniques & Interventions
https://positivepsychology.com/grief-counseling/

11 Impactful Benefits of Grief Counseling
https://www.talkspace.com/blog/benefits-of-grief-counseling/

15 Ways to Give Back in Honor of Your Loved One
https://www.milanomonuments.com/blog/11-ways-to-give-back-in-honor-of-your-loved-one

16 Ideas for Creating New Holiday Tradition After a Death
https://whatsyourgrief.com/creating-new-tradition-after-a-death/

20 Unique Memorial Service Ideas *https://www.celestis.com/blog/20-unique-memorial-service-ideas/*

8 Ways to Manage Milestones After Losing a Loved One
https://www.goldsteinsfuneral.com/8-ways-to-manage-milestones-after-losing-a-loved-one/

9 DIY Projects to Honor a Loved One's Memory
https://www.milanomonuments.com/blog/diy-projects-to-honor-a-loved-ones-memory

A force for change: Coping with grief through activism
https://www.cnn.com/2017/11/11/health/force-for-change-grief-coping/index.html

Anger with God: Grappling with God Amidst Life's Greatest ...
https://bradhambrick.com/angerwithgod/

Complicated Grief: What It Is, Symptoms & Treatment
https://my.clevelandclinic.org/health/diseases/24951-complicated-grief

Continuing Bonds: Shifting the Grief Paradigm
https://whatsyourgrief.com/continuing-bonds-shifting-the-grief-paradigm/

Coping with anniversaries and reminders
https://www.cruse.org.uk/understanding-grief/managing-grief/coping-with-anniversaries-and-reminders/

Creating a Memorial Space in Your Home
https://www.myfarewelling.com/article/creating-a-memorial-space-in-your-home

Depression vs. grief - *MedicalNewsToday*
https://www.medicalnewstoday.com/articles/depression-vs-grief

Find a Grief Therapist
https://www.psychologytoday.com/us/therapists?category=grief

Grief and Bereavement: When a Child Dies
https://www.stanfordchildrens.org/en/topic/default?id=grief-and-bereavement-90-P03048

Grief meditation: How to use mindfulness to heal after loss
https://www.calm.com/blog/grief-meditation

Grieving the Loss of a Sibling *https://www.cancer.net/coping-with-cancer/managing-emotions/grief-and-loss/grieving-loss-sibling*

How Journaling Can Help You Grieve | Diversus Health
https://diversushealth.org/mental-health-blog/how-journaling-can-help-you-grieve/

How the Death of a Child Can Impact a Marriage
https://ftm.aamft.org/how-the-death-of-a-child-can-impact-a-maeeiage

How to Find New Purpose in Life After Child Loss
https://unlockingjoy.com/finding-purpose-after-loss/

How to Host a Virtual Circle: *https://healingcirclesglobal.org/how-to-host-a-virtual-circle/*

How To Interpret Signs & Symbols From Friends & Family *http://theworldofdoug.com/blog/signsandsymbolsfromthedead*

How to Plan a Personalized Memorial Service - Tulip Cremation *https://www.tulipcremation.com/how-to-plan-a-personalized-memorial-service.html*

How to Set Up a Memorial Fund *https://charitysmith.org/how-to-set-up-a-memorial-fund/*

How to Take Care of Yourself While Grieving *https://together.stjude.org/en-us/for-families/bereavement/self-care-during-grief.html*

Loss of Adult Child: How to Cope with Grief *https://www.silversneakers.com/blog/loss-adult-child-how-to-cope-grief/*

Loss of an Adult Child - Support Groups *https://www.cancercare.org/support_groups/195-loss_of_an_adult_child*

Meaning-Making Coping Methods among Bereaved Parents *https://www.ncbi.nlm.nih.gov/pmc/articles/PMC8533093/*

Planning a Memorial Service: A Step-by-Step Guide *https://www.myfarewelling.com/article/planning-a-memorial-service-a-step-by-step-guide*

Resilience Psychology and Coping with Grief *https://drarielleschwartz.com/resilience-psychology-and-coping-with-grief/*

Self-Care During Grief: How to Create Your Plan *https://www.eterneva.com/resources/self-care-during-grief-tips*

Spirituality for Coping with the Trauma of a Loved One
https://www.ncbi.nlm.nih.gov/pmc/articles/PMC8853234/

Support and bereavement groups - Mayo Clinic
https://www.mayoclinic.org/patient-visitor-guide/support-groups#:~:text=Benefits%20of%20support%20groups&text=A%20group%20can%20provide%20and,after%20a%20loved%20one's%20death
.

Support and bereavement groups - Mayo Clinic
https://www.mayoclinic.org/patient-visitor-guide/support-groups#:~:text=Benefits%20of%20support%20groups&text=Moreover%2C%20support%20and%20bereavement%20groups,mood%20and%20decrease%20psychological%20distress.

Supporting Grieving Siblings: What You Should Know
https://childrensroom.org/supporting-grieving-siblings/

The Compassionate Friends Non-Profit Organization for Grief
https://www.compassionatefriends.org/

The Compassionate Friends Non-Profit Organization for Grief
https://www.compassionatefriends.org/

The Healing Power of Memorial Keepsakes
https://www.lindquistmortuary.com/the-healing-power-of-memorial-keepsakes

The Healing Power of Storytelling After a Loved One's Death
https://warmpathways.com/the-healing-power-of-storytelling-after-a-loved-ones-death/

The physical symptoms of grief and loss: What to know
https://www.medicalnewstoday.com/articles/the-physical-symptoms-of-grief-and-loss

The Role of Extended Family Relations and Rituals in Family
https://journals.sagepub.com/doi/10.1177/10541373211034632

The therapeutic effectiveness of using visual art modalities
https://www.ncbi.nlm.nih.gov/pmc/articles/PMC5798551/

Understanding the Physical Symptoms of Grief
https://www.healthline.com/health/grief-physical-symptoms

Volunteerism: Service as Grief Support
https://www.laurelbox.com/blogs/news/volunteerism-service-while-grieving

What to Know About the Anger Stage of Grief
https://www.verywellmind.com/the-anger-stage-of-grief-characteristics-and-coping-5295703

When No One Understands: Communication & Grief
https://www.griefincommon.com/blog/when-no-one-understands-communication-grief/

While We're Waiting – Faith-Based Retreats for Bereaved Parents
https://whilewerewaiting.org/